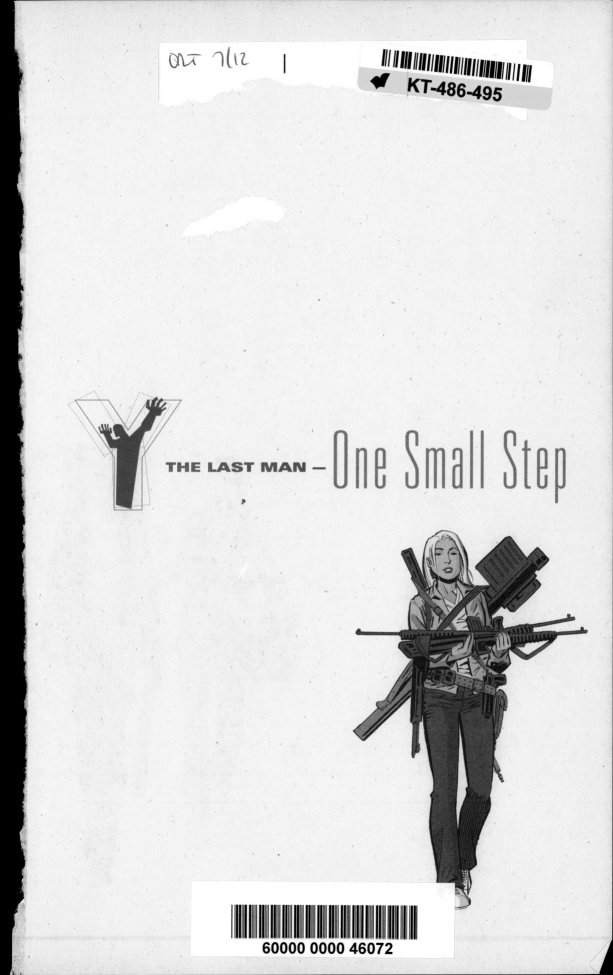

THE LAST MAN — One Small Step

THE LAST MAN – One Small Step

Brian K. Vaughan
Writer

Pia Guerra
Paul Chadwick
Pencillers

José Marzán, Jr.
Inker

Pamela Rambo
Colorist

Clem Robins
Letterer

J.G. Jones
Original series covers

Y: THE LAST MAN created by Brian K. Vaughan and Pia Guerra

DC Comics, 1700 Broadway, New York, NY 10019
A Warner Bros. Entertainment Company.
Printed in the USA. Fifth Printing.
ISBN: 978-1-4012-0201-9
Cover illustration by J.G. Jones.

Certified Fiber Sourcing
www.sfiprogram.org
Fiber used in this product line meets the sourcing requirements of the SFI program. www.sfiprogram.org SGS-SFICOC-0130

ONE MAN'S STORY...

The plague struck without warning and without mercy, all across the globe. Every mammal on Earth that bore a Y chromosome died in a matter of seconds. Out of billions of animals, only two were spared — a human named Yorick Brown, and his pet monkey, Ampersand. Why they survived is a mystery.

In the aftermath of this apocalypse, Yorick and Ampersand set out from Brooklyn to contact Yorick's mother, a U.S. congresswoman. After making their way down a devastated eastern seaboard, they found her in Washington, D.C., struggling to keep the remains of the U.S. government intact. The appearance of the last man (and monkey) provided a newly installed President with fresh hope for the future of the human race, and Yorick soon found himself on a mission to track down the cloning expert Dr. Allison Mann to help her try to prevent the species' extinction.

After briefly crossing paths with a group of man-hating radicals called the Daughters of the Amazon, Yorick and Ampersand made it to Dr. Mann's lab in Boston — accompanied by Agent 355, a member of a shadowy government security force known as the Culper Ring. There they found the bioengineer in a state of anguish, convinced that her cloning experiments had caused the plague. But while Yorick had been looking for Dr. Mann, another group was looking for *him* — a team of Israeli commandos, the most accomplished female soldiers in the world, far from home and pursuing their own agenda. After missing the Last Man in the lab, they decided to burn it to the ground.

With few other options available to them, Yorick, Ampersand, 355 and Dr. Mann set out for California to retrieve the backups of Dr. Mann's data. After bribing their way into a boxcar heading west, however, the group was set upon by thieves and forced to abandon the train outside Marrisville, Ohio — a town settled by the population of a women's prison.

Marrisville proved to be an oasis of stability in a countryside filled with anarchy, but that calm was shattered with the arrival of the Daughters of the Amazons, who had tracked down Yorick with the help of their newest member — his sister, Hero. Threatening to destroy the town unless the Last Man was turned over for execution, the Amazons' leader was instead cut down herself by the woman who had found Yorick unconscious next to the railroad tracks — an act of bravery that she paid for with her life, courtesy of Hero's archery skills. Reeling from what his sister had become, Yorick left her with the remaining Amazons in Marrisville's reopened prison, and continued west with his companions.

Now, as their train rolls slowly across the plains, a hijacked Black Hawk helicopter follows from the east, quickly closing the distance between the Last Man and a grimly determined team of Israelis. And two hundred and twenty miles above them all, three desperate humans prepare for their return voyage from space — a one-way trip that, if successful, could triple the number of men on Earth.

ROAD
JG JONES 03

**Marquand, Missouri
Now**

IS IT IMPORTANT? I'M BROODING.

JUST WONDERING IF I COULD BORROW THAT LIGHTER OF YOURS.

I WAS GOING THROUGH ABANDONED CARS FOR SUPPLIES AND I...FOUND SOMETHING.

WHAT KIND OF SOMETHING?
HALF A' PACK.
WHEN THE HELL DID YOU START *SMOKING*, 355?

WHEN A PLAGUE OF BIBLICAL PROPORTIONS KILLED EVERY MAN EXCEPT FOR *YOUR* HAIRY ASS?

FAIR ENOUGH.
CAN I BUM ONE OFF YOU?

SORRY, 'RICK. THE PRESIDENT ORDERED ME TO *PROTECT* YOU, NOT TO SULLY YOUR PINK LUNGS.
SUIT YOURSELF.
HOPE THE CULPER RING TAUGHT YOU HOW TO RUB TWO STICKS TOGETHER.

IF YOU EVER TELL YOUR MOTHER ABOUT THIS, I'LL KILL YOU MYSELF.
GOD YOU'RE EASY...

"FUCK COMMUNISM"?

WHAT ARE YOU, A COSSACK?
OH, THE ENGRAVING?
IT'S FROM THIS THING I READ BACK IN HIGH SCHOOL, A, UH...A "GRAPHIC NOVEL." YOU KNOW, LIKE A COMIC BOOK?

THEY CAN SAY "FUCK" IN COMIC BOOKS?

I GUESS.
JEEZ, THEY NEVER SAID STUFF LIKE THAT IN *SUPERMAN*.

SUPERMAN'S JUST MAKE-BELIEVE, 355.
IN THE REAL WORLD...

...I'M THE STRONGEST MAN ON EARTH.

One Small Step

Chapter One

BRIAN K. VAUGHAN PIA GUERRA
Writer/Co-Creators/Penciller

JOSE MARZAN, JR., Inker

Clem Robins, Letterer **Pamela Rambo**, Colorist
Zylonol, Separator **J.G. Jones**, Cover Artist
Steve Bunche, Editor

Y: THE LAST MAN CREATED BY BRIAN K. VAUGHAN AND PIA GUERRA

KOFF--KOFF--
AHWUHH--
KOFF--

YEAH, YOU'RE A REGULAR MAN OF STEEL, ALL RIGHT.
IS HE *SMOKING?*

HOW THE FUCK IS HE SUPPOSED TO SAVE THE PLANET WHEN HE'S CANCER-RIDDEN AND...AND *IMPOTENT?*

RELAX, DOC, IT'S JUST--
WHATEVER, BREAK'S OVER. THEY'VE APPARENTLY FINISHED REPAIRING THE LITTLE ENGINE THAT COULDN'T.

AND GET THIS ANIMAL AWAY FROM ME. IT DEFECATED IN MY *MEDICAL BAG*.
COME ON, AMPERSAND... BEFORE MRS. HYDE'S TRANSFORMATION IS COMPLETE.

GO EASY ON HIM, DR. MANN. HE'S STILL NOT OVER WHAT HAPPENED BACK IN MARRISVILLE.
355, IS THERE SOMETHING GOING *ON* BETWEEN YOU TWO?
WHO, ME AND...?

EW, NO!
THIS ISN'T *POST-COITAL*, IF THAT'S WHAT YOU'RE SUGGESTING.
WELL, IT'S JUST...BACK IN OHIO, YOU *SAID* SOMETHING. WHEN YOU WERE UNCONSCIOUS. YOU SAID...

FORGET IT.
PROBABLY JUST THE ANESTHESIA TALKING.
TRUST ME, DOCTOR, MY ONLY INTEREST IN YORICK IS KEEPING HIM OUT OF *TROUBLE*...

HEY, YOU!

ME?
YEAH... WHAT'S THAT BEARD MADE OUT OF?

IT'S SPIRIT GUM AND, UH... HORSEHAIR.
OH.
THOUGHT SO. YOU SHOULD REALLY TRY USING YOUR *OWN* HAIR. SAVE SOME CLIPPINGS NEXT TIME YOU GET IT CUT. LOOKS MORE NATURAL.

YEAH.
THAT'S WHAT PEOPLE KEEP TELLING ME.

SO, YOU GOT A GIRL-FRIEND?
OR ARE YOU A WORKING GIRL LIKE ME?

GIRLFRIEND.
WE'RE ENGAGED, ACTUALLY... MORE OR LESS.
GOOD, I WAS AFRAID YOU WERE GONNA TAKE ALL OF MY CUSTOMERS ON THIS LINE.

SERIOUSLY, YOUR LADY'S LUCKY TO HAVE SOMEONE AS DEDICATED AS YOU. BIND THOSE BREASTS A LITTLE TIGHTER AND YOU'LL ALMOST BE PASSABLE.
...THANKS?

ANYWAY, HAVE A SAFE TRIP.
KEEP AN EYE OUT FOR AMAZONS!
WILL DO.

ER AH HA
YOU AND ME, LITTLE BUDDY...ADRIFT IN AN OCEAN OF ESTROGEN.

ROCKS AND TREES, ROCKS AND TREES...
I CAN'T WAIT TO GET OUT OF THIS GODDAMN CABOOSE FOR GOOD.

DON'T GET TOO EXCITED, YORICK. EVEN WHEN WE DO REACH SAN FRANCISCO, IT'S NOT LIKE WE'LL HAVE TIME FOR CRACKED CRAB AND JET SKIS.
I HAVE HUNDREDS OF TESTS TO PERFORM ON YOU...PRESUMING MY LATE DAUGHTER'S EMBRYONIC CELLS ARE STILL INTACT FOR COMPARISON.
DAUGHTER? I THOUGHT THE CLONE YOU GAVE BIRTH TO WAS A MALE.

WHAT?
OF COURSE. THAT'S WHAT I--

THUNK
THE HELL...?

SOUNDS LIKE SOMETHING HIT OUR ROOF.
I'LL CHECK IT OUT.

I'M COMING WITH YOU.
NO!

IF HE TRIES TO FOLLOW ME, DO WHAT WE DISCUSSED.
I'M ON IT.

WHAT THE *FUCK*?

OH, YOU GUYS *STINK*.

IF ANYBODY'S THERE, I'M COMING UP!
AND I'M ARMED!

NO! PLEASE!
IT TOOK ME DAYS TO GET BACK ON TRAIN! I AM TRYING TO GET TO MAN!

I'M AFRAID THAT WON'T BE POSSIBLE.
THINK

YOU DO NOT UNDER-STAND!
I TRAVEL ALL THE WAY TO THE STATES WITH MY--
DON'T!

EHN!

NOW DROP THE RIFLE OR I'LL--
FUCKING PIZDA!
Soloman's Starr

UHN!
NN!
KYAH!

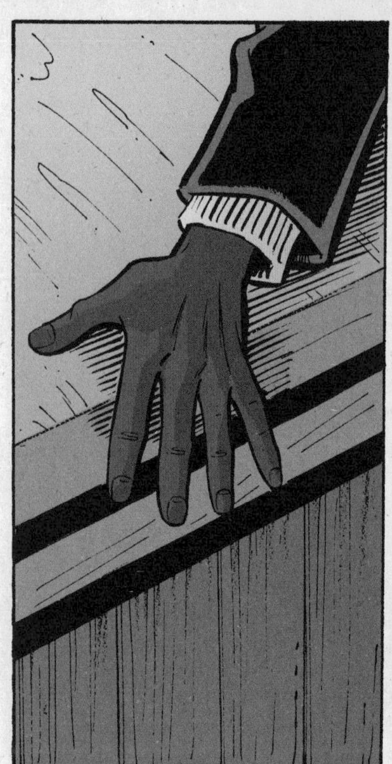

OOF!

FUCK!

JESUS CHRIST, HERE WE GO...

...AGAIN?

USE MY HELP, PLEASE!

I SAVE LIFE AND YOU LET ME INSIDE YOUR TRAIN, DA?
THAT MEDAL... HOW THE HELL DID YOU GET A GOLD STAR?

I WAS GOOD LITTLE GIRL IN SCHOOL.

BUT THAT'S RESERVED FOR HEROES OF THE RUSSIAN FEDERA--
NO MORE KICKING, NO MORE QUESTIONS. WE ARE FRIENDS AND EVEN, OKAY?
3SS!

UM... EVERYTHING COOL UP HERE?

GODDAMMIT, YORICK.
HOW...?

HEY, I RECOGNIZE HER.
SHE'S THAT STOWAWAY THEY THREW OFF THE TRAIN BACK IN MARRISVILLE.
WHO... WHO IS THIS MAN?

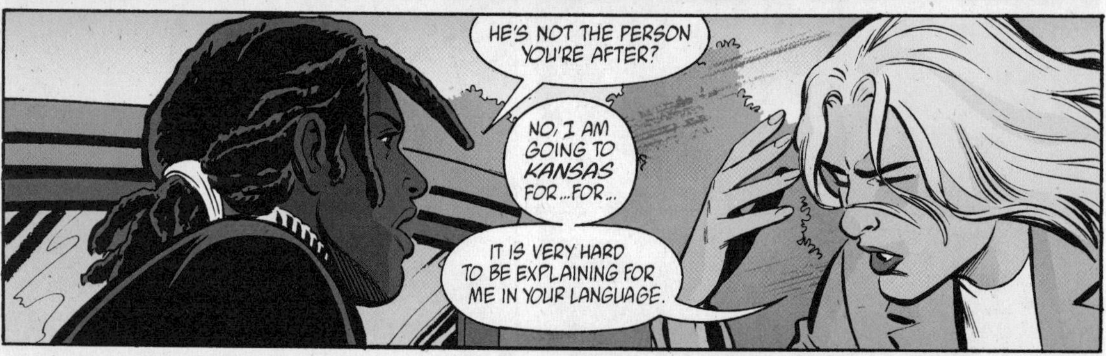
HE'S NOT THE PERSON YOU'RE AFTER?
NO, I AM GOING TO KANSAS FOR...FOR...
IT IS VERY HARD TO BE EXPLAINING FOR ME IN YOUR LANGUAGE.

<THEN TRY IT IN YOUR TONGUE.>
<YOU SPEAK RUSSIAN?>

<NOT FOR LONG TIME.>
<MY GRAMMAR IS A LITTLE, um... FROGGY?>

‹THANK CHRIST! I SOUND LIKE A FUCKING *RETARD* WHEN I TRY TO SPEAK ENGLISH.›
‹SLOW DOWN. WHO *IS* YOU?›

‹MY NAME'S NATALYA ZAMYATIN.›
‹I WAS SENT BY WHAT'S LEFT OF THE GOVERNMENT TO RETRIEVE OUR COUNTRY'S ONLY LIVING MALE, A COSMONAUT ON BOARD THE INTERNATIONAL SPACE STATION.›
‹*WHAT?*›
HEY, COMRADES, CAN SOMEONE TRANSLATE THIS OR--

‹FOR MONTHS, HE'S BEEN TRAPPED INSIDE THE I.S.S. WITH TWO OF YOUR ASTRO-NAUTS, ONE MALE AND ONE FEMALE.›
‹HOW CAN YOU BE SURE HE'S STILL ALIVE?›

‹WELL, WE LOST HAM CONTACT A FEW WEEKS AGO, BUT MY PEOPLE HAVE TALKED TO BOTH MEN SINCE JULY, SO WE KNOW THEY SURVIVED THE PLAGUE.›
‹THEY'VE BEEN WAITING FOR *NASA* TO SEND A SHUTTLE TO RESCUE THEM...BUT HOUSTON APPARENTLY DOESN'T HAVE THE RESOURCES TO MAKE THAT HAPPEN.›
‹THEN HOW ARE *YOU* PLANNING TO GET UP THERE?›

‹I'M NOT.›
‹*THEY'RE* COMING DOWN *HERE*.

YOU'VE HEARD THE HORROR STORIES, RIGHT? THE SOYUZ ISN'T A LIFE-BOAT, IT'S A *DEATHTRAP*.
WELL, WE'RE OBVIOUSLY NOT BEING SENT THAT LIMO WE REQUESTED, AND I'D RATHER BITE IT IN SOME CORNFIELD THAN SUFFOCATE INSIDE THIS JUNKHEAP.

EVEN IF WE *DON'T* CRASH, HOW CAN WE BE SURE THAT WHATEVER KILLED ALL THE MEN DOWN THERE WON'T KILL *YOU* THE SECOND WE LAND?
WE CAN'T, BUT WE'RE TAKING EVERY PRECAUTION POSSIBLE, CIBA.
WE'RE GOING DOWN IN SUITS, AND VLAD'S CONTACT IS SUPPOSED TO BE WAITING AT OUR E.L.Z. TO ESCORT US TO THE HOT SUITE AS SOON AS WE BLOW THE LATCH.
TRUE, COMMANDER...

...BUT FIRST WE MUST SURVIVE REENTRY.
SPEED LIMIT 1750

VLAD. SORRY, I THOUGHT YOU WERE STILL IN THE HEAD, TRIMMING THAT NEW SOUP STRAINER OF YOURS.
LISTEN, WHAT I WAS SAYING... IT HAS NOTHING TO DO WITH MY FAITH IN YOU AS A PILOT.
NOR SHOULD IT BE MY ABILITIES WHICH CONCERN YOU.

BECAUSE OF CHEMICAL DEGRADATION IN HYDRAZINE FUEL, SOYUZ WAS DESIGNED TO BE STORED IN SPACE FOR MAXIMUM OF SIX MONTHS.
OUR VESSEL HAS NOT BEEN REPLACED IN MORE THAN NINE.
SURE, BUT WE'VE GOT SOME WIGGLE ROOM WITH THOSE NUMBERS, RIGHT?

RUSSIAN ENGINEERS ARE NOT BIG ON "WIGGLE ROOM," SIR.

SO HOW CAN WE TELL IF THE PROPELLANT'S CORRODED ANY OF OUR SOYUZ'S DEEP PLUMBING?
ONLY ONE WAY TO KNOW FOR CERTAIN...
...IF OUR CABIN BURSTS INTO FLAMES WHEN WE ENTER ATMOSPHERE.

THIS JUST KEEPS GETTING BETTER AND BETTER...

Marquand, Missouri
Two Hours Later

I HAVE AN ENTIRE BRIGADE OF THE ISRAELI DEFENSE FORCES SCOURING THE COORDINATES YOU GAVE US, AND STILL NO SIGN OF THIS "YORICK" CHARACTER.

FOR YOUR SAKE, STRANGER, I PRAY YOU HAVE NOT SENT US ON ANOTHER WILD-GOOSE CHASE.

DID YOU KNOW SHAKESPEARE COINED THAT PHRASE?
WHAT?
"WILD-GOOSE CHASE," I MEAN.

ORIGINALLY, IT DESCRIBED AN UNPREDICTABLE PATH TAKEN BY ONE INDIVIDUAL AND FOLLOWED BY ANOTHER...ENDING WHEN THE FIRST IS INEVITABLY CAUGHT.
MY SPOUSE LOVED TO POINT OUT THAT ITS MODERN USAGE IS REALLY A PESSIMISTIC MISINTERPRETATION OF--

ENOUGH! FOR MONTHS, YOU HAVE BORED ME WITH THIS PEDANTIC NONSENSE, WHILE GIVING ME NO USEFUL INFORMATION. I HAVE YET TO EVEN LEARN YOUR REAL NAME!
ALTER, BE PATIENT. I'VE TOLD YOU EVERYTHING YOU NEED TO KNOW TO FIND THE LAST MAN ON EARTH, AND YOU'RE CLOSE.
I'M NOT SURE HOW SECURE THIS FREQUENCY IS, SO I CAN'T SAY MORE THAN--

THAT EXCUSE IS NO LONGER ACCEPTABLE. GIVE ME A REASON TO CONTINUE TRUSTING YOU, OR I AM TAKING MY TROOPS BACK TO TEL AVIV.
NOW, FOR THE LAST TIME, WHO ARE YOU?
GOOD LORD, ISN'T IT OBVIOUS, ALTER?

I'M THE ONLY MOTHER WHO STILL HAS HER SON.
GONE FISHIN'

THE LAST MAN ON EARTH IS YOUR *CHILD?*

UNLESS I *IMAGINED* THOSE TWENTY-SIX HOURS I WAS IN LABOR.
MY NAME IS REPRESENTATIVE JENNIFER BROWN. I'M--

REPRESENTATIVE? YOU'RE A U.S. *CONGRESSWOMAN?* THEN, WHY THE HELL DID YOU ASK *ISRAEL* FOR HELP? YOUR OWN MILITARY IS--
--STILL IN DISARRAY, ALTER, AS YOU'VE SEEN. I KNEW *YOU* WERE THE ONLY WOMAN WITH THE SKILLS AND RESOURCES TO RETRIEVE MY SON.
YOUR PREDECESSOR WAS...HE WAS A DEAR *FRIEND* OF MINE. LIEUTENANT-GENERAL YEHUDA ALWAYS SPOKE VERY HIGHLY OF YOU.

BESIDES, I'VE RUN OUT OF *AMERICANS* I CAN TRUST.

EXPLAIN.
I ASSURE YOU, THE NETWORK MY PEOPLE CREATED IS SECURE. OUR FREQUENCY IS--
YES, YES, FINE. IT HAPPENED SHORTLY AFTER MY SON LEFT WASHINGTON...

I LEARNED THE ORGANIZATION THAT HAD SWORN TO PROTECT YORICK WASN'T MADE UP OF ALTRUISTIC SERVANTS OF THE EXECUTIVE BRANCH, AS OUR NEW PRESIDENT HAD LED ME TO BELIEVE.
THIS "CULPER RING" IS ACTUALLY A GROUP OF THUGS AND... AND ASSASSINS, A GLORIFIED DIRTY TRICKS CREW. FOR DECADES, THEY'VE COMMITTED ATROCITIES FOR CORRUPT ADMINISTRATIONS.
AND YOU NOW SUSPECT THAT THIS GROUP HAS, WHAT, KIDNAPPED YOUR SON?

ONE OF THEIR AGENTS, YES... "355". I'M NOT SURE WHAT HER AGENDA IS, BUT I KNOW THAT SHE RECENTLY TRANSPORTED YORICK TO YOUR CURRENT LOCATION.
YOU ORIGINALLY SAID THEY WERE LOOKING FOR SOME GENETICIST IN BOSTON. WHAT MAKES YOU THINK YOUR SON AND HIS CAPTOR ARE NOW HERE IN MISSOURI?

THERE'S A CHANCE THEY MAY HAVE JUST BEEN PASSING THROUGH, ALTER. SEE, AN ASSOCIATE IN THE SECRET SERVICE ENCOURAGED ME TO PLANT A TRACKING DEVICE ON YORICK BEFORE HE LEFT.
WITH THE SATELLITES DOWN, SHE'S BEEN TRIANGULATING USING WHATEVER RADIO TOWERS ARE AVAILABLE, AND IT SOMETIMES TAKES A FEW HOURS TO GET A LOCK.
EITHER WAY, HOW CAN YOU BE CERTAIN THIS BEACON HASN'T BEEN FOUND AND REMOVED?

BECAUSE WE HID IT INSIDE YORICK'S MONKEY.

HIS WHAT?

GRR AKAK
One Small Step
Chapter Two
BRIAN K. VAUGHAN PIA GUERRA
Writer/Co-Creators/Penciller
JOSE MARZAN, JR., Inker
Clem Robins, Letterer Pamela Rambo, Colorist
Zylonol, Separator J.G. Jones, Cover Artist
Steve Bunche, Editor
Y: THE LAST MAN CREATED BY BRIAN K. VAUGHAN AND PIA GUERRA

Oldenbrook, Kansas
Ten Hours Later

THIS IS INSANE, 355! WE'RE GOING TO ABANDON OUR ORIGINAL PLAN BECAUSE SOME GIRL WITH A BULLSHIT STORY LANDS ON OUR *ROOF*?

WE'RE NOT ABANDONING ANYTHING, DR. MANN. WE'RE TAKING A TEMPORARY DETOUR.

MY STORY IS NO BULL-SHIT!

GOD, THIS IS GONNA BE *AWESOME*...

IF WHAT NATALYA SAYS IS TRUE, A SOYUZ ESCAPE VESSEL IS ABOUT TO LAND WITH ONE FEMALE AND TWO MALES INSIDE. TWO *LIVING* MALES.
THOSE ASTRONAUTS ARE GOING TO NEED MY PROTECTION AND YOUR MEDICAL ATTENTION.
AND MY DISARMING WIT!

SERIOUSLY, DOC, LET YOUR UNFEELING CYBORG BRAIN RELEASE A LITTLE SEROTONIN FOR ONCE. THIS IS A MIRACLE!
NO, THIS IS A *SHAM*.

ANYONE WHO'S WATCHED AN HOUR'S WORTH OF DISCOVERY CHANNEL KNOWS THAT THE SOYUZ ALWAYS LANDS IN THE *KAZAKH STEPPES* OUTSIDE OF RUSSIA...
...NOT IN THE MIDDLE OF SOME ALFALFA FIELD IN BUMFUCK, KANSAS.

NO, KAZAKHSTAN IS *NO* POSSIBLE!
AKTAU MAKE *POISON*! AKTAU BRING DEATH!
WAIT, REWIND. WHAT'S *AKTAU*?

IT'S A NUCLEAR POWER PLANT.

NO. NOT ANOTHER CHERNOBYL.
WORSE. MY GOVERNMENT THINK POSSIBLE ONE MILLION WOMAN DEAD. NUMBERS WILL BECOME MORE WHEN CANCER BLOWS TO RUSSIA.
OF COURSE, IF I'M NO ABLE TO BRING BACK OUR COSMONAUT IN SAFETY, MY COUNTRY HAS MORE TO WORRY ABOUT FOR FUTURE THAN DISEASE.

‹NATALYA, I THOUGHT KAZAKHSTAN TOOK THEIR REACTOR, UM, WHAT'S THE RUSSIAN WORD FOR...?›
‹"OFFLINE"? YEAH, SO DID WE. BUT BEFORE THE PLAGUE, MALE OFFICIALS WERE APPARENTLY OPERATING IT IN SECRET FOR PROFIT.›
‹WHILE RUSSIA WAS WORKING ITS ASS OFF TO SHUT DOWN ALL OF OUR PLANTS, KAZAKHSTAN'S CORE WAS MELTING DOWN. ONE LAST "FUCK YOU" FROM A CORRUPT BUREAUCRACY.›

JESUS, WHAT A NIGHTMARE. ALL THOSE PEOPLE LIVED THROUGH THE PLAGUE...ONLY TO DIE IN SOME STUPID ACCIDENT?
IS HORRIBLE TRAGEDY, YES, BUT AT LEAST WOMEN HAD EACH OTHER, YORICK.
MY COUNTRY HAS SAYING, "EVEN DEATH IS BEAUTIFUL, IF YOU ARE NOT ALONE."

YOU SAY SO.

355, IF THAT HAPPENS TO ONE OF OUR REACTORS--
IT WON'T. MY COLLEAGUES HAVE BEEN DECOMMISSIONING PLANTS FOR MONTHS NOW, ALL ACROSS THE COUNTRY.
TRUST ME, THE CULPER RING IS TAKING CARE OF EVERYTHING.

International Space Station
Now

UHN!

YOU WANT VIRUS TO INFECT *ME* AT LANDING SO *YOU* CAN BE ONLY MAN ON EARTH! YOU--

DECK
OOF!

IF I WANTED TO KILL YOU, I'D GET IT OVER WITH *UP HERE,* YOU FUCKING--
HEY!

IN THIS HAND, I HAVE ENOUGH DIAZEPAM TO PUT A T-REX IN A COMA.

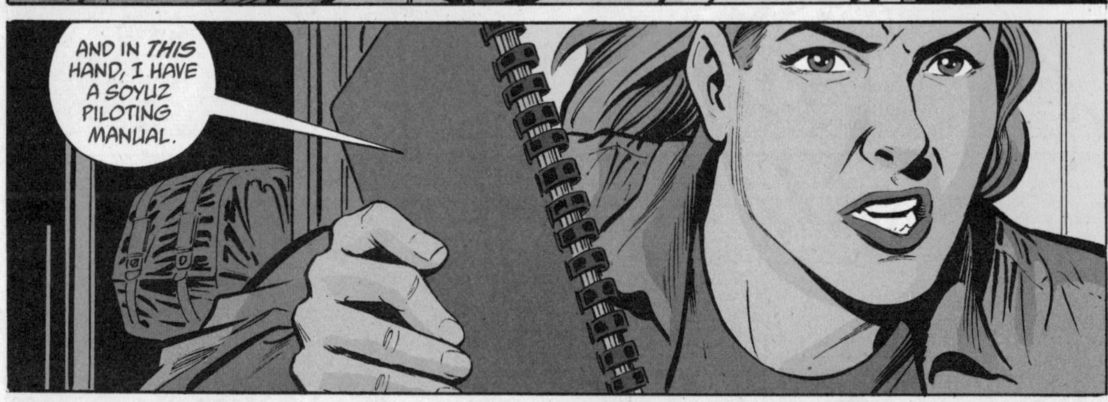
AND IN THIS HAND, I HAVE A SOYUZ PILOTING MANUAL.

NOW, I'M NOT SURE IF I CAN MAKE IT BACK TO EARTH ALONE...

...BUT I WANT YOU BOTH TO KNOW THAT I'M WILLING TO TRY.

COMMANDER, YOU...YOU MUST FORGIVE ME.
I HAVE NO IDEA WHAT OVER-CAME ME.
YEAH, I'M I'M SORRY TOO, VLAD.

IT MUST BE THE OXYGEN DEPRIVATION, CIBA.
IT'S MAKING US *PSYCHOTIC*.

3,298 TRIPS AROUND THAT GOD-DAMN BLUE BALL.
TWICE AS MANY SHITTY POKER GAMES.
WELL, LET'S TRY TO KEEP IT TOGETHER, GENTLE-MEN. I KNOW IT FEELS LIKE WE'VE BEEN STUCK IN THIS THING TOGETHER *FOREVER*...

...BUT IN A FEW HOURS, IT'LL ALL BE OVER.

ONE WAY OR ANOTHER.

OKAY, BUT EVEN IF THESE THEORETICAL SPACEMEN REALLY *DID* ESCAPE THE PLAGUE, HOW DO WE KNOW IT WON'T AFFECT THEM ONCE THEY TOUCH DOWN?
WE DON'T. THIS IS WHY MY BOSSES ORDER SOYUZ TO LAND BY YOUR COUNTRY'S NEW, HOW DO YOU SAY...
IS IT "WARM ROOM"?

OUR *HOT SUITE?* THE RUSSIANS *KNEW* ABOUT IT?
K.G.B. IS DEAD, FRIEND, BUT OUR INTELLIGENCE IS NOT.

UM, I REALIZE MY USELESS B.A. IS SHOWING ...BUT WHAT THE HELL IS A HOT SUITE?
IT'S A GROUP OF LEVEL FOUR BIO-SAFETY ROOMS, SUPPOSEDLY IMPERVIOUS TO ANY INFECTIOUS AGENTS FROM THE OUTSIDE WORLD AND BLAH, BLAH, BLAH.
I KNEW THERE WAS ONE AT FORT DETRICK, BUT WE'RE IN THE MIDDLE OF *NOWHERE*.

THE GOVERNMENT HID A MASSIVE FACILITY OUT HERE FOR HIGH-RANKING OFFICIALS TO RETREAT TO IN CASE OF BIOLOGICAL ATTACKS TO MAJOR CITIES.
THEY *DID?* DO WE KNOW IF ANY DUDES WERE INSIDE THIS THING *BEFORE* THE PLAGUE HIT?

NOPE... BUT I GUESS WE'RE ABOUT TO FIND OUT.
VRRMM

‹FORGET ABOUT REFUELING, PILOT.›
‹WE'RE NOT FAR FROM THE NEW COORDINATES THE AMERICAN PROVIDED.›
‹MY, MISSOURI YESTERDAY AND KANSAS TODAY? LET US PRAY WE HAVE NOT ONCE AGAIN "NARROWLY MISSED" THE LAST BOY ON EARTH.›

‹SADIE, A MOMENT OF YOUR TIME, PLEASE.›

‹IF YOU EVER AGAIN TAKE THAT TONE WITH ME IN FRONT OF MY SOLDIERS...›

‹...I WILL HAVE TO ASK YOU TO *STEP OUTSIDE*.›

<I APOLOGIZE, LIEUTENANT-GENERAL, BUT I'M BEGINNING TO SUSPECT THAT YOU DRAGGED US ON THIS SCAVENGER HUNT SIMPLY BECAUSE YOU'D GROWN *BORED* WITH PEACE IN ISRAEL.>
<YOU'RE WRONG.>
<I'M DOING WHAT'S BEST FOR OUR PEOPLE.>

<WORKING AS AN ERRAND GIRL FOR SOME AMERICAN POLITICIAN?>
<NO, SEEING THAT THE ONLY FUNCTIONING *SPERM FACTORY* DOESN'T FALL INTO THE HANDS OF THE ENEMY.>

<YOU KEEP USING THAT TERM, "THE ENEMY.">
<BUT YOU TAUGHT ME THAT EUPHEMISMS ARE ONLY FOR THOSE WHO FEEL *GUILT* ABOUT WHAT THEY'RE DESCRIBING. IF YOUR CONSCIENCE IS CLEAR, ALTER, SAY WHAT YOU MEAN...>

<ARABS.>

‹THAT'S NOT WHAT THIS IS ABOUT. MY ONLY CONCERN IS *TERROR*. HAMAS, ISLAMIC JIHAD...›
‹THOSE GROUPS DON'T NEED *MEN* TO BLOW UP BUSES, ALTER! A...A *FEMALE* SUICIDE BOMBER KILLED MY BROTHER-IN-LAW!›

‹THEN YOU UNDERSTAND THE NEED FOR VIGILANCE.›
‹NO, I DON'T! THERE HASN'T BEEN A SINGLE BOMBING SINCE THE MEN DIED!›
‹AND I INTEND TO KEEP IT THAT WAY.›

‹HOW, BY REUNITING SOME RANDOM YOUNG MAN WITH HIS *MOTHER?*›
‹DON'T BE AN IDIOT, SADIE. I HAVE NO INTENTION OF RETURNING YORICK TO THAT GULLIBLE SIMPLETON.›
‹THE WAY SHE LOOKS AFTER HER SON, THAT WOULD BE TANTAMOUNT TO HANDING HIM DIRECTLY TO *HEZBOLLAH*.›

‹THEN...WHAT *ARE* YOU PLANNING TO DO WITH THE BOY?›
‹SET US DOWN HERE, PILOT.›
‹WE'LL GO IN THE REST OF THE WAY ON FOOT.›

‹IT'S IMPORTANT TO MAINTAIN THE ELEMENT OF SURPRISE.›

SO.
YOU, ehh... CHILD OF POLITICS?
WELL, MY MOM'S IN WASHINGTON, IF THAT'S WHAT YOU MEAN.
THIS IS HOW YOU STILL LIVE? SHE GIVES YOU SOME KIND OF ANECDOTE?
AN ANTIDOTE? NO, WHY WOULD SHE HAVE A...
WAIT, YOU DON'T THINK THE AMERICAN GOVERNMENT CAUSED THE PLAGUE, DO YOU?
MY SISTERS IN MILITARY SUSPECT POSSIBLY. I'M NO SURE WHAT TO THINK, YORICK.
SWELL, WE LOSE ALL THE MEN, BUT AT LEAST WE GET THE GODDAMN COLD WAR BACK.
ANYWAY, I'M STILL GLAD WE FOUND YOU, NATALYA.
YOU BROUGHT THE FIRST POTEN-TIALLY GOOD NEWS I'VE HEARD SINCE MY LIFE TURNED INTO A BAD OUTER LIMITS EPISODE.
COME, SMALL PART OF YOU IS SADDENED YOU MIGHT NOT BE AS... AS SPECIAL NOW, DA?

NYET. HELL, NYET.
THOSE GUYS UP THERE WERE FUCKING HEROES EVEN BEFORE THE PLAGUE HIT. THEY'RE MUCH BETTER QUALIFIED TO SAVE MANKIND THAN SOME SOCIALLY RETARDED WHITE KID.
DON'T GET ME WRONG, I STILL WANT TO DO WHATEVER I CAN TO HELP, BUT MY MOTTO'S ALWAYS BEEN, "WITH LITTLE POWER COMES LITTLE RESPONSIBILITY."
AND THAT'S NOT ABOUT BEING A SLACKER, MIND YOU. IT'S ABOUT KNOWING YOUR LIMITATIONS. I MEAN, I CAN BARELY DO A CHIN-UP.
THE ONLY SHIT I'VE EVER BEEN GOOD AT INVOLVES CHINESE FINGER CUFFS AND... AND MILK CAN ESCAPES. MOST OF THE TIME, I JUST FUCK STUFF UP.
EVERYONE THINKS THEY KNOW HOW TO "FIX" THE WORLD, BUT WE'D ALL BE A LOT BETTER OFF IF SOME OF US JUST STAYED OUT OF THE WAY... YOU KNOW?
FORGIVE ME, YORICK, MY ENGLISH IS NOT FOR CRAP. I HAVE NO IDEA WHAT YOU JUST SAY.
BUT IS NICE TO HEAR MAN'S VOICE AGAIN.

UM, WHY ARE YOU UNBUTTON-ING...?

YOUR COUNTRY SO BEAUTIFUL, BUT TOO FUCK-ING HOT.
ALWAYS THE HEAT...
NATALYA, I DON'T MEAN TO BE RUDE, BUT COULD YOU, UH, STAY AS CLOTHED AS POSSIBLE AROUND ME?

<LORD, I NEVER THOUGHT I WOULD MISS MOSCOW.>
<THE WAY THE MEN'S BODIES LITTERED RED SQUARE ...THEY LOOKED LIKE CHILDREN, MAKING ANGELS IN THE SNOW.>

<AND I REMEMBER FINDING YOU, SWEET RODYA. THE IMAGE OF YOUR FACE, FROZEN IN MY MIND...>
ALSO, WOULD YOU MIND NOT MUTTERING TO YOURSELF IN RUSSIAN? YOUR ACCENT IS DISTURB-INGLY SEXY.
IT'S JUST, I'VE GOT THIS GIRL I'M TRY-ING REALLY HARD TO STAY LOYAL TO, BUT THE FLESH IS WEAK, AS THEY SAY, AND I'M ONLY--

SCREECH
UNF!
FWAP

SORRY ABOUT THAT.
BUT I THINK WE'RE HERE.

YOU SURE ABOUT THAT, OLD MacDONALD?

IT'S A *SECRET* INSTALLATION, YORICK.

IT'S NOT SUPPOSED TO LOOK LIKE THE PENTAGON.

YEAH, BUT A *BARN?*

THAT'S WHERE BANDITS GO TO HIDE BEFORE THEY INEVITABLY GET *SHOT* TO DEATH.

JOHN WILKES BOOTH WAS KILLED INSIDE A BARN.

SERIOUSLY, HAVEN'T WE BEEN THROUGH ENOUGH SIEGES ALREADY?

WELL, SEEING AS WE'RE NEITHER OLD-TIMEY OUT-LAWS OR REBEL ASSASSINS, I THINK WE'RE IN THE CLEAR.

AND SINCE WHEN DID *YOU* START ENCOURAGING MAGIC LAD?

SORRY, THREE-FIFTY, BUT I'M STILL FINDING ALL OF THIS A LITTLE HARD TO SWALLOW.

NO, IS TRUE! IS EXACTLY AS F.S.B. DESCRIBE TO ME!

HEIDI, HIT HIM WITH THE DECON SPRAY!

THE WHA--

GGLUHWAR

STOP!
M'E VAS POKHORONIM!

WHOA! EASY, THELMA AND LOUISE!
IT'S JUST DECONTAM-INATE.

WE HAVE TO GET THIS MAN TO A STAGING AREA!
NO YOU DON'T. THE KID'S TOTALLY IMMUNE. WE'RE NOT HERE ABOUT HIM.

WHAT THE HELL DO YOU MEAN?
SHE MEANS DON'T PUT AWAY THE E.T. GEAR YET, LADIES.
SPTOO

YOU'RE ABOUT TO GET SOME OUT-OF-TOWN VISITORS.

YORICK BROWN...

<...WE MEET AT LAST.>

Maitland
Darlington
McFall
Mound City
Rosendale
Rea
Napier
Oregon
Troy
Wathena
Everest
Huron
Atchison
Summit
Butler
City
JG JONES 03

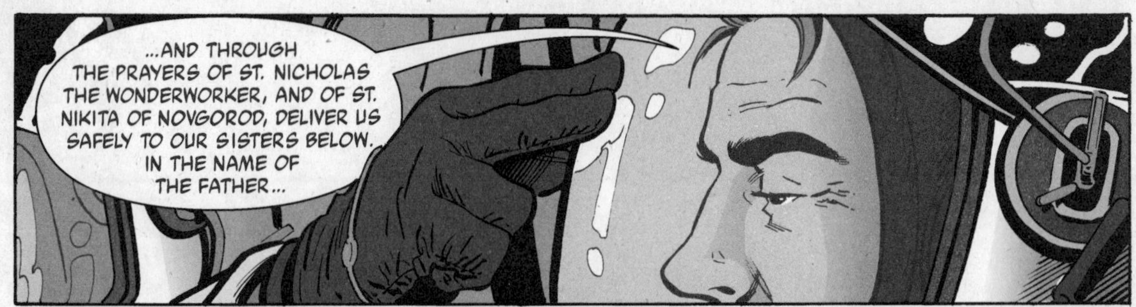
...AND THROUGH THE PRAYERS OF ST. NICHOLAS THE WONDERWORKER, AND OF ST. NIKITA OF NOVGOROD, DELIVER US SAFELY TO OUR SISTERS BELOW. IN THE NAME OF THE FATHER...

...AND OF THE SON...

...AND OF THE HOLY GHOST.

OR DO WE SAY HOLY *SPIRIT?* I...I HAVEN'T DONE THIS SINCE I WAS *EIGHT.*
I *LOVE* YOU, CIBA. YOU, *TOO,* VLAD.
I'M UNDOCKING NOW, COMMANDER. WE'RE FREE.

AMEN.
One Small Step
Chapter Three
BRIAN K. VAUGHAN PIA GUERRA
Writer/Co-Creators/Penciller
JOSE MARZAN, JR., Inker
Clem Robins, Letterer
Pamela Rambo, Colorist
Zylonol, Separator
J.G. Jones, Cover Artist
Zachary Rau, Assistant Editor
Will Dennis, Editor
Y: THE LAST MAN CREATED BY
BRIAN K. VAUGHAN AND PIA GUERRA

Oldenbrook, Kansas
Now

WHAT ARE YOU *TALKING* ABOUT?

OH, IT'S A *LITTLE RASCALS* THING. I DON'T REALLY HATE--

ASTRONAUTS? ARE COMING *HERE? HOW?* WHO *ARE* YOU PEOPLE?

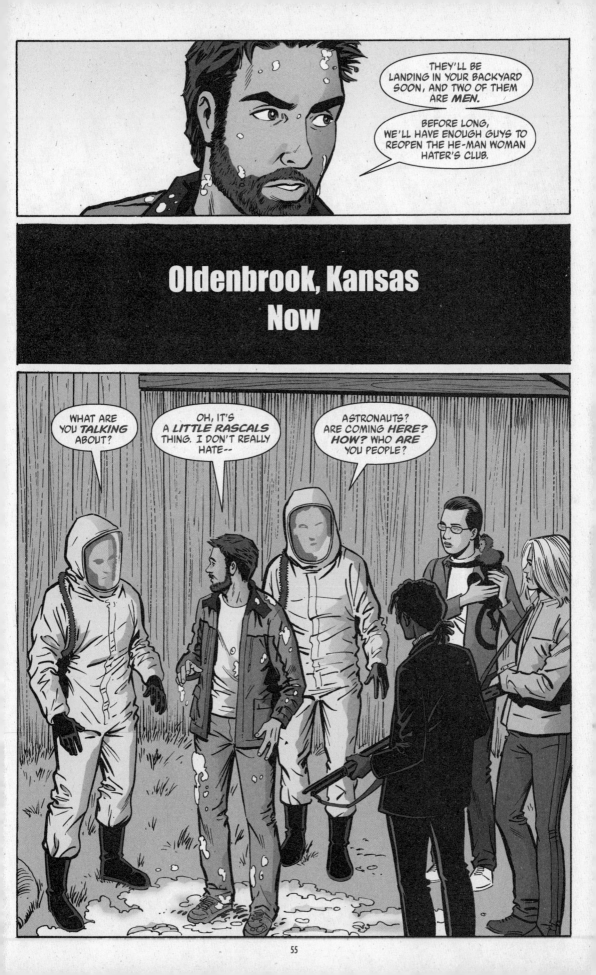

I'M AGENT 355. I WORK FOR THE UNITED STATES GOVERNMENT.
THE BOY YOU JUST HOSED DOWN IS YORICK BROWN. WE DON'T KNOW HOW OR WHY HE SURVIVED THE PLAGUE.
BUT WE DO KNOW THAT HE IS A **MAN,** NOT A BOY.

NATALYA ZAMYATIN, SENT BY THE RUSSIANS TO RETRIEVE THEIR COSMONAUT.
DOBRAHYE OOTRAH.

AND AMPERSAND'S TOY OVER THERE IS DR. MANN, A BIOENGINEER OUT OF--

THE DR. MANN?
DR. **ALLISON** MANN?

DID... DID YOU MAKE THEM?
THEY'RE NOT CLONES, IDIOT.
THEY'RE TWINS.

DOCTOR, MY NAME'S HEATHER HARTLE. THIS IS MY SISTER, HEIDI. WE'RE GENETICISTS.
YOUR JAMA PIECE ON ORGAN BLUEPRINTING MADE ME CRY.
I'M GUESSING YOU'RE NOT SQUATTERS HERE.

NO, WE'RE EMPLOYEES OF THE HOT SUITE.
THE ONLY EMPLOYEES. THE REST OF THE STAFF TOOK OFF MONTHS AGO.
YOU MEAN, THERE AREN'T ANY MEN ALIVE IN THERE?

NONE OF THE POLITICIANS WHO HAD THIS AS THEIR DESIGNATED C.O.G. SITE EVER SHOWED UP. AND ONLY WOMEN EVER WORKED HERE.
MALES HAVE... TROUBLE WITH THE ISOLATION.

FUCKING...
FUCK.

I AM SORRY, YORICK, BUT YOUR HOPE IS NOT BEING GONE YET.

IS WHAT HE SAID *TRUE?*
THERE ARE STILL PEOPLE ALIVE ON THE SPACE SHUTTLE?
YOUR GUESS IS AS GOOD AS MINE. I'M JUST GOING ALONG FOR THE RIDE.

LISTEN, WE NEED TO SECURE THIS FACILITY BEFORE THE *SOYUZ* TOUCHES DOWN. IF YOU REFUSE TO LET US INSIDE, MY EXECUTIVE S.C.I. CLEARANCE AUTHORIZES ME TO--

RELAX, LADY. HOUSING PEOPLE IS OUR RAISON D'ETRE. WE'VE BEEN WAITING A *YEAR* FOR SOME-THING LIKE THIS.
YEAH, MI CASA, ETC.
I'D LOVE TO RUN A FEW TESTS ON THE BOY.

JESUS, KILL ME NOW...

TSE'ELON, LO!

‹WHAT THE HELL ARE YOU DOING? DO YOU WANT TO COMPROMISE OUR POSITION?›
‹I WANT TO STOP YOU FROM OFFING THE LAST FUCKING MAN ON EARTH!›

‹CALM DOWN, SADIE, YOU KNOW THE SCOPES ARE MORE POWERFUL THAN OUR SHIT BINOCULARS. OR HAVE YOU FORGOTTEN EVERY-THING I TAUGHT YOU ABOUT RECONNAISSANCE?›
‹RECONNAIS-SANCE? SO YOU WEREN'T GOING TO SHOOT HIM?›
‹DO YOU THINK I'M COMPLETELY MAD?›

‹THEN...WHAT ARE WE GOING TO DO WITH THE KID, ALTER?›
‹WE'RE TAKING HIM TO ISRAEL.›

‹IF WE CAN FIND A WAY TO DO SOMETHING ABOUT HIS CAPTORS.›
‹THIS "CULPER RING" GIRL YORICK'S MOTHER WARNED US ABOUT SEEMS TO HAVE PICKED UP SOME KIND OF MERCENARY, LOOKS LIKE EX-SPETSNAZ.›
‹WAIT, WE'RE GOING TO KIDNAP YORICK FROM HIS KIDNAPPERS?›

‹YOU'RE THE ONE WHO'S SO CONCERNED ABOUT THE "FUTURE OF ISRAEL," NO?›
‹OF COURSE, BUT HOW ARE YOU GOING TO CONVINCE SOME AMERICAN GOY TO REPOPULATE OUR HOMELAND?›

‹PERHAPS WE'LL LOCK HIM IN A ROOM WITH SEVENTY-TWO VIRGINS. I'VE HEARD THAT'S SOME MEN'S IDEA OF HEAVEN.›
‹WHY ARE YOU TALKING ABOUT HIM LIKE HE'S A TERRORIST? HE'S AN INNOCENT BOY!›

‹NONE OF US IS INNOCENT.›

‹OH, SAVE THAT NONSENSE FOR THE NEW GIRLS.›
‹WHAT ARE YOU PLAYING AT HERE? IF WE STEAL YORICK, THE AMERICANS WILL GO TO WAR TO GET HIM BACK.›
‹WE SHOULD BE SO LUCKY.›

‹WHAT DOES THAT MEAN?›
‹YOU SAW WHAT HAPPENED BACK AT THE TEMPLE MOUNT A FEW MONTHS AGO, DIDN'T YOU? BETWEEN OUR OWN PEOPLE? THE RIOTING? THE FISTFIGHTS?›
‹YEAH, WELL, THE ULTRA-ORTHODOX WOMEN INTERPRET THE PLAGUE A LITTLE DIFFERENTLY THAN THE REST OF US. BIG SURPRISE.›
‹WHAT DOES THAT HAVE TO DO WITH YORICK?›

‹THE FIGHTING DIDN'T BEGIN IN EARNEST UNTIL THE I.D.F. ... SEDATED OUR ARAB NEIGHBORS.›
‹AS SOON AS WE REMOVED ALL OF ISRAEL'S EXTERNAL THREATS, THE INTERNAL CONFLICT THAT'S BEEN SIMMERING FOR YEARS FINALLY CAME TO A BOIL.›
‹THE SAME THING WILL HAPPEN TO OUR ALLIES IN THE STATES SOON ENOUGH.›
‹WITHOUT AN OUT-SIDE "EVIL" FOR ITS CITIZENS TO HATE, POOR WILL EVENTUALLY TURN AGAINST RICH, WHITE AGAINST BLACK, AND--›
‹WHAT ARE YOU SUGGESTING, THE ONLY WAY TO PROTECT PEACE IN OUR NATIONS IS TO INVENT A WAR? WHAT THE HELL KIND OF PLAN IS THAT?›

‹A VERY OLD, VERY RELIABLE ONE.›

MAN, THIS PLACE IS LIKE SMALLVILLE UPSTAIRS, FORTRESS OF SOLITUDE DOWNSTAIRS.
YOU CLEAN UP GOOD, YORICK.
COME, ENJOY HOT MUSH IN BAG WITH ME.

OH, GOD, NOT M.R.E.s. I LIVED OFF THOSE THINGS FOR A WEEK ON MY WAY TO D.C. THE SUPER-MARKETS HAD ALL BEEN RANSACKED, BUT I FOUND SOME DEAD GUY IN PENNSYLVANIA WITH AN OLD Y2K BUNKER IN HIS BACKYARD.
FAT LOT OF GOOD PREPARING FOR THE WORST DOES, HUH? EVERY BOY SCOUT THEY TAUGHT TO "BE PREPARED" IS A CORPSE NOW.
THANK-FULLY, THAT'S ALSO THE GIRL SCOUTS' MOTTO.

I WAS A BROWNIE.

HEATHER AND HEIDI JUST GAVE US A NICKEL TOUR OF THE LOWER LEVEL, AND THEY SEEM *PERFECT.*
THE SPACE CADETS CAN THEORETICALLY SURVIVE DOWN THERE FOR YEARS, UNTIL WE'RE SURE THE PLAGUE'S DISSIPATED.
OR UNTIL DR. MANN COMES UP WITH SOME KIND OF VACCINE.

NO! NOT ACCEPTABLE!
UNITED NATIONS CHARTER SAY, "IF, OWING TO ACCIDENT, DISTRESS, EMERGENCY OR UNINTENDED LANDING, THE PERSONNEL OF A SPACECRAFT LAND IN TERRITORY UNDER THE JURISDICTION OF A CONTRACTING PARTY, THEY SHALL BE SAFELY AND PROMPTLY RETURNED TO REPRESENTATIVES OF THE LAUNCHING AUTHORITY!"

WHAT THE...? *COOKIE MONSTER* SPEAKS BETTER ENGLISH THAN YOU. WHEN THE HELL DID YOU LEARN ALL THAT?
I HAVE LONG BOAT RIDE TO STATES FOR MEMORIZING.

WE HAVE NO INTENTION OF TAKING YOUR MAN *HOSTAGE,* NATALYA. WE'RE JUST HOLDING HIM FOR OBSERVATION.
FOR NOW, I DON'T WANT THE BOYS VENTURING BEYOND THIS SECTOR. YORICK AND AMPERSAND MAY BE IMMUNE TO WHATEVER CAUSED THIS, BUT THERE'S A CHANCE THEY'RE STILL--

BOOOM

WAS THAT...?
SOYUZ.

YOU SAID IT'S NOT SUPPOSED TO BE ENTERING THE ATMOSPHERE FOR ANOTHER THREE HOURS!
THEY MUST BE MOVE UP WINDOW TO AVOID STORM OR--

WHATEVER. GRAB YOUR GEAR, NATALYA.
LADIES, YOU'RE AT STANDBY ON THE AIRLOCKS DOWNSTAIRS.

DOCTOR, KEEP AN EYE ON YORICK.
I'D NEVER DO ANYTHING TO FUCK THIS UP, 355.

SCOUT'S HONOR.

‹SHOULD WE BE WORRIED ABOUT THAT SMOKE?›
‹NOT NECESSARILY. THE R.S.C. EGGHEADS TOLD ME THE SOFT-LANDING ENGINES MIGHT SINGE PART OF THE FIELD. THE CAPSULE CAN TAKE THE HEAT.›

‹I'M A LITTLE CONCERNED ABOUT THE PLACEMENT, THOUGH. PILOTING THOSE TIN CANS ISN'T AN EXACT SCIENCE, BUT THEY'RE ABOUT THREE VERSTS OUTSIDE THE TARGET ZONE.›
‹VERSTS?›
SORRY, IN THE ENGLISH, VERST IS ALMOST ABOUT, EHH... ONE KLICK.

‹A KLICK? THAT'S A REAL WORD? I THOUGHT THEY ONLY USED THAT IN BAD VIETNAM MOVIES.›
‹ARE YOU HIGH? OF COURSE IT'S REAL. A KLICK IS ONE KILOMETER... THAT'S .62 MILES IN AMERICAN.›
‹I CAN HANDLE METRIC, SMARTASS. BUT I'VE BEEN PART OF A PARAMILITARY ORGANIZATION SINCE I WAS SIX-TEEN, AND I'VE NEVER HEARD ANYONE USE--›

MOTHERFUCK.

SHTO ETA?
WHAT IS THIS?
A JOHN DEERE.

DA, BUT WHY IS IT EXPLODING FOR NO REASON?
THE BARN.

GET BACK TO THE BARN!

HEY, HAVE YOU SEEN PICTURES OF EITHER OF THESE NASA DUDES, DOC?
MAYBE YOU'LL MAKE A LOVE CONNECTION.
I FIND THAT HIGHLY UNLIKELY, YOR--

MR. BROWN, YOU'RE WITH US NOW.

WHO THE FUCK ARE *YOU?*
MOVE AND YOU'RE DEAD!
WAIT!

I...I SURRENDER.
JUST DON'T HURT ANYONE ELSE. PLEASE.
YORICK...

TAKE HIM, LADIES. GET THE MONKEY, TOO.

YOU SURE ABOUT THAT?
SHE HAS *AIDS.* AND SHE *BITES.*
AR OH

‹MA'AM?›
‹FINE, LEAVE THE DAMN ANIMAL WITH THE WOMAN.›
‹JUST MOVE!›

‹YOU HEAR THAT? SOUNDS LIKE A **HELICOPTER...** AMERICAN MILITARY?›
‹IS IT COMING OR GOING?›

‹CAN'T TELL.›
‹ALL RIGHT, DON'T SHOOT ANYONE UNTIL WE KNOW THE SCORE.›

‹BUT THOSE ASSHOLES SCAMMED US!›
‹WE DON'T KNOW **WHAT'S** GOING ON, GOD-DAMMIT! JUST KEEP YOUR SAFETY ON UNTIL--›

‹ISRAELIS?›

‹GUN!›
BLAM

UHN!
NO!

‹WE HAVE WHAT WE CAME FOR, PULL OUT!›
‹ALTER, HOLD ON! SELTZER AND KLARSFELD ARE STILL AT THEIR POST!›
‹GOOD, THEY CAN PROVIDE GROUND COVER UNTIL WE'RE CLEAR!›

YALLA!

YORICK!
GET YOUR HANDS WHERE I CAN SEE--

BLAM

KLICK
‹FUH... FREEZE!›

PLEASE, NO...
KLICK
KLICK
KLICK

AHHHHH!
BLAM
BLAM
BLAM

UHF!

LET GO OF THE GUN!
LO! BEVAKASHA! TAKE...TAKE ME TO MY HOTEL!

I'LL KILL YOU!
HOW MUCH DOES THIS COST PLEASE! WHERE IS THE LIBRARY! WHICH SUBWAY--

STUPID.
TRISTA... PYATDESYAT...

THREE HUNDRED, IS... IS YOU DEAD?

NATALYA. ARE YOU...?
‹I'LL ⸗EHN⸗ LIVE. I'M SO SORRY. CAN'T BELIEVE I FUCKING PASSED OUT. LIKE IT'S MY FIRST TIME GETTING SHOT. ARE THE OTHERS--›

‹I DON'T KNOW, BUT I THINK THEY GOT YORICK.›
‹A RADIO. ONE OF THEM HAD A RADIO...›
‹THERE.›

WHOEVER THIS IS, TURN YOUR CRAFT AROUND AND BRING THE MALE BACK NOW.
⸗KZACK⸗
AGENT 355, IS IT...?

...I CAN GIVE YOU **TWO** MEN IN EXCHANGE.

JESUS, MY GAUGES ARE BURIED SO DEEP IN THE RED, SOME OF THEM HAVE GONE **GREEN** AGAIN.

YOU THINK THE WOMEN WILL THROW A PARADE FOR US, VLAD?

I SHOULD HOPE SO, SIR. ONE TO RIVAL GAGARIN'S IN '61.

I KNOW WHY YOU BOYS ARE JOKING, BUT I'M TELLING YOU THAT YOU ***SHOULD*** BE STRESSED. IF WE CAN'T KEEP SHOCK NEUTRALIZATION ONLINE--

WHO DO YOU THINK THEY'LL HAVE WAITING FOR US DOWN THERE, VLAD? SOME OF THOSE SEXY NURSES?

PERHAPS A FEW OF YOUR CHEERLEADERS.

One Small Step
Chapter Four
I DON'T THINK SO.
BRIAN K. VAUGHAN PIA GUERRA
Writer/Co-Creators/Penciller
JOSE MARZAN, JR., Inker
Clem Robins, Letterer Pamela Rambo, Colorist
Zylonol, Separator J.G. Jones, Cover Artist
Zachary Rau, Ass't Editor Will Dennis, Editor
Y: THE LAST MAN CREATED BY
BRIAN K. VAUGHAN AND PIA GUERRA

Oldenbrook, Kansas
Now

SHUT THE HELL UP, NATALYA!
‹WHAT RIGHT DO YOU HAVE TO SURRENDER MY MAN? I TRAVELED ACROSS A GODDAMN OCEAN TO RETURN OUR ONE FUCKING COSMONAUT TO--›

IF YOU DON'T SHUT YOUR MOUTH, YOU'RE GOING TO HAVE A SECOND BULLET IN YOU. AND I GUARANTEE I'M A BETTER SHOT THAN THEY WERE.

IS EVERY-THING ALL RIGHT, AGENT?
LISTEN CAREFULLY, MY TEAM AND I ARE GOING TO PICK UP THE MEN AT THEIR EMERGENCY LANDING ZONE AND BRING THEM BACK TO THE FACILITY WHERE YOU STOLE YORICK.
YOU'LL MEET US THERE LATER TONIGHT, AND WE'LL MAKE THE TRADE.

YOU ASSUME THAT I THINK YOUR STORY IS TRUE.
BESIDES, EVEN IF IT WERE, WHY WOULD YOU SACRIFICE TWO GROWN MEN FOR ONE SCRAWNY BOY?
HEY! ASSHOLE! THIS BAG ISN'T SOUNDPROOF!

BECAUSE, I'M... I'M IN LOVE WITH HIM.

SHE'S WHAT?

WELL... THIS IS FINALLY STARTING TO MAKE SENSE.

FINE THEN, WE WILL MEET YOU TONIGHT. BUT IF YOUR SPACESHIP FAILS TO APPEAR...YOU WILL NEVER SEE YOUR BOYFRIEND AGAIN.
ALTER OUT.

‹PILOT, SET US DOWN!›

‹WE HAVE WORK TO DO...›

‹YOU DESPERATE FUCKING IDIOT. THEY'LL NEVER GIVE YOU YORICK BACK!›
‹THEY'RE GOING TO TAKE MY COUNTRY'S ONLY MAN FOR THEMSELVES AND SLAUGHTER THE REST OF US! AND FOR WHAT, SOME STUPID CRUSH?›
DON'T BE DENSE, NATALYA. I'M NOT LETTING THEM TAKE YOUR COSMONAUT, AND I'M DEFINITELY NOT IN LOVE WITH YORICK.

I ONLY SAID THAT TO GET THEM BACK HERE.
‹SORRY, MY ENGLISH MUST BLOW...I THOUGHT YOU JUST SAID THAT YOU'RE DELIBERATELY LURING AN ENTIRE PLATOON BACK TO THE PEOPLE WHO KILLED TWO OF THEIR SOLDIERS!›
355!

DR. MANN!
THEY... THEY GOT YORICK.
I KNOW. IS EVERYONE OKAY?

I'LL LIVE, BUT THOSE THUGS TOSSED HEATHER AND HEIDI A PRETTY GOOD BEATING ON THEIR WAY INSIDE THE COMPOUND.
DID...DID WE JUST GET RAIDED BY ISRAELIS?
WHY? I MEAN, WE'RE JEWISH!

WE'LL WORRY ABOUT MOTIVES LATER. RIGHT NOW, I NEED YOU TO FIX NATALYA'S SHOULDER AS BEST YOU CAN.
WE HAVE WORK TO DO...

IT'S A TRAP!

SHE...SHE MADE UP THAT BULLSHIT ABOUT *NASA* DUDES TO *TRICK* YOU. LET'S JUST GET OUT OF HERE AND PROCEED WITH THE TORTURING OR WHATEVER.
<THE MORE HE OBJECTS, THE MORE I *BELIEVE* THE AMERICAN GIRL'S ASSERTION.>
<I'M NOT SURE, ALTER. IT STILL SOUNDS PREPOSTEROUS TO ME.>

<EITHER WAY, A BOY IN THE HAND IS WORTH TWO IN THE BUSH, NO?>
<SO WHAT, YOU'RE GOING TO HOLD ON TO THE BOY *AND* MAKE A PLAY FOR THE ASTRONAUTS?>
<SADIE, IF ANY-ONE OTHER THAN ISRAEL ACQUIRES MALES, OUR NATION LOSES THE LEVERAGE AND POSITION THAT COME WITH HAVING YORICK.>

<I'M DOING WHAT I HAVE TO DO.>
<BUT YORICK'S PROBABLY *RIGHT* ABOUT THE AMERICANS SETTING A TRAP INSIDE THAT BARN!>
<THAT'S WHY WE'RE TAKING THE FIGHT *OUTSIDE.*>

<NAIM, I WANT YOU TO LEAD THE REST OF THE UNIT BACK TOWARDS THE FACILITY WE STORMED. FROM A SAFE DISTANCE, SHADOW THE AMERICANS TO THE LANDING ZONE.>
<THE CULPER RING AGENT HAS ONE OF OUR HANDHELDS, SO MAINTAIN RADIO SILENCE UNTIL I CONTACT YOU WITH FURTHER INSTRUCTIONS.>
BEHATZLACHA!

‹I SHOULD GO WITH THEM, ALTER. THOSE GIRLS ARE BARELY FIELD RATED, AND NAIM ISN'T EXACTLY LEADERSHIP MATERIAL.›
‹I WANT YOU WITH ME, SADIE.›
‹IF THIS 355 IS SMART, SHE'S ALREADY DISPATCHED PART OF HER TEAM TO LOOK FOR YORICK. IT WILL TAKE US BOTH TO GUARD HIM.›

UM, I MAY NOT SPEAK HEBREW, BUT IT'S PRETTY CLEAR WHEN YOU'RE TALKING ABOUT ME. ALL I HEAR IS, "GIBBERISH GIBBERISH YORICK GIBBERISH."

YOU'RE A HEARTBEAT AWAY FROM BEING GAGGED, MR. BROWN.
AND I THINK THAT I'M STARTING TO UNDERSTAND THIS BLACK SACK ROUTINE, TOO.
IT'S NOT ABOUT KEEPING ME IN THE DARK, RIGHT? IT'S ABOUT HELPING YOU PRETEND THAT I'M JUST AN OBJECT AND NOT A--

IF I REMOVE IT, WILL YOU PROMISE TO STOP BLABBERING?
OW. PUPILS... CONSTRICTING.

‹SADIE, KEEP A CLOSE EYE ON OUR GUEST.›
APPARENTLY, HE FANCIES HIMSELF QUITE THE ESCAPE ARTIST.

OOO, AM I SUPPOSED TO BE IMPRESSED BY YOUR SCARY "INTEL"?
EVERYONE WHO'S READ MY AWARD-WINNING NEWSLETTER KNOWS WHAT I DO.
NO, YOU'RE SUPPOSED TO BE IMPRESSED BY THE HANDCUFFS YOU'VE BEEN TRYING TO FREE YOURSELF FROM FOR THE LAST HOUR.

THEY WERE DESIGNED BY MOSSAD TO BE ONE HUNDRED PERCENT UNPICKABLE.
THE ONLY PALESTINIAN EVER TO BREAK OUT OF MEGIDDO PRISON STILL HAD TO SAW OFF HIS LEFT HAND TO GET OUT OF--
ARE YOU TAUNTING ME WITH A MANIACAL DEATHTRAP? WHAT ARE YOU, A BATMAN VILLAIN?

SERIOUSLY, I THOUGHT YOU PEOPLE WERE SUPPOSED TO BE THE GOOD GUYS.
NO MATTER WHAT STUPID SHIT YOUR PRIME MINISTER EVER DID, MY PARENTS WERE ALWAYS HUGE SUPPORTERS OF ISRAEL. I MEAN, DO YOU EVEN KNOW WHO MY MOTHER IS?

<BETTER THAN YOU DO, I SUSPECT.>
WHAT DID YOU JUST SAY? DID YOU JUST INSULT MY MOM? SAY IT IN ENGLISH, G.I. JANE, I DARE YOU!

<CUFF HIM TO ONE OF THE CHAIRS INSIDE THE COPTER.>
<IF HE REFUSES TO BE SILENT, KNOCK HIM UNCONSCIOUS.>

YOU SURE WE'RE IN THE RIGHT PLACE?
POSITIVE. ALL WE HAVE TO DO NOW IS WAIT.
I STILL DON'T UNDERSTAND WHY I HAD TO COME ALONG, 355.

I TOLD YOU, WE NEED THE TWINS ON CALL BACK AT THE HOT SUITE.
BUT NATALYA--
--IS DOING WHAT I ASKED HER TO DO, DOCTOR. IF MY PLAN WORKS, WE'LL BE ABLE TO HOLD ON TO THE ASTRONAUTS AND GET YORICK BACK.

AND IF IT DOESN'T?

‹IS THAT HER, NAIM? IS SHE THE ONE WHO KILLED SELTZER AND KLARSFELD?›
‹HOW THE HELL AM I SUPPOSED TO KNOW? BESIDES, WE'RE NOT HERE TO GET REVENGE.›
‹NOT YET, ANYWAY...›

HEY, YOU SPEAK ENGLISH?
BE QUIET.

I'LL TAKE THAT AS A YES. LISTEN, YOU'RE OBVIOUSLY NOT CRAZY ABOUT THIS WHOLE CAMPAIGN. IT'S WRITTEN ALL OVER YOUR FACE.
MAYBE YOU THINK YOU'RE JUST FOLLOWING ORDERS HERE...BUT DON'T FORGET HOW THAT EXCUSE WENT OVER AT NUREMBERG.
IF YOU ARE TRYING TO WIN MY FAVOR, I WOULD ADVISE YOU AGAINST COMPARING ME TO PEOPLE WHO KILLED MY GREAT GRAND-FATHER.

OH.
BESIDES, THAT WOMAN TOOK A BULLET FOR ME IN HEBRON. HOW...HOW COULD I JUST BETRAY HER NOW? HOW COULD I--
SADIE!

GET OUT HERE. SOMETHING'S HAPPENING.

WHAT'S GOING ON? I WANNA SEE!
BEN ZSONA.

I DON'T BELIEVE IT.
IT'S RAINING MEN.

HALLELUJAH.

‹SADIE, GIVE ME SOME GROUND COVER WHILE I READY THE **S.A.M.**›
‹SAM?›

‹AN OLD FRIEND.›

‹YOU'RE... YOU'RE **JOKING,** RIGHT?›

‹WE DON'T HAVE TIME TO BE PRECIOUS ABOUT THIS, SADIE. WE ONLY NEED ONE MAN TO ENSURE OUR NATION'S SECURITY. OTHERS WOULD JUST BECOME LIABILITIES.›
‹I ASKED YOU TO STAY WITH ME BECAUSE I KNOW YOU'RE--›

‹PUT IT DOWN.›

‹...INTERESTING.›
‹I PRESUME YOU STILL REMEMBER THE PUNISHMENT FOR ***TREASON?***›
‹THIS HAS TO STOP, ALTER. I'M BEGINNING TO REALIZE THAT A NEVER-ENDING BATTLE IS JUST A...A WAR WITHOUT ***WINNERS.***›

‹YOU'RE MAKING A VERY BAD DECISION.›
‹MAYBE, BUT AT LEAST I'M FINALLY MAKING ONE. THAT'S SOMETHING I SHOULD HAVE DONE A LONG TIME--›

KRAK

‹I AM SORRY, LITTLE ONE.›

‹YOU ARE A GOOD GIRL...›

‹...BUT SOMETIMES WE MUST DO TERRIBLE THINGS FOR PEACE.›

NO!

MAYBE I DON'T KNOW HOW TO GET OUT OF ***THESE*** THINGS...
...BUT I DO KNOW HOW TO GET OUT OF A FUCKING ***CHAIR!***
NNN!

HOLY SHIT!
WHAT WAS THAT?

‹YOU HEARD HER! SHOOT TO KILL!›

‹THEY'RE IN THE GRASS! FAN OUT AND--›

AHN!
NAIM?

‹MY LEG!›
‹WHAT'S HAPPENING?›
AFF!

‹WHO THE HELL IS FIRING?›

POOR DUMB KIDS.
LIKE HITTING FISHES IN BUCKET...

LISTEN UP! I'M SURE AT LEAST ONE OF YOU SPEAKS ENGLISH, SO SPREAD THE WORD!
AT THE COUNT OF THREE, I AM GOING TO STAND BACK UP. IF YOU HAVE ALL DROPPED YOUR WEAPONS AND PUT YOUR HANDS IN THE AIR, NO ONE ELSE WILL BE HARMED.
THIS IS NEVER GOING TO WORK, 355! THERE ARE LIKE A DOZEN OF THEM AND ONLY TWO OF--

IF YOU TRY TO KILL ME, YOU MIGHT SUCCEED, BUT MY SNIPER WILL STOP AIMING FOR APPENDAGES AND START HITTING **FACES.** THE CHOICE IS YOURS!
ONE... **TWO...**

THREE.

COLLECT THEIR WEAPONS AND PUT THEM INTO ZIP TIES, DOCTOR. NATALYA HAS YOUR BACK, SO DON'T BE SCARED.
WOW.

ISRAELI COMMAND, THIS IS AGENT 355. YOUR GREED JUST **INVALIDATED** OUR DEAL.
I'M CURRENTLY HOLDING YOUR ENTIRE REGIMENT HOSTAGE, AND WON'T RETURN THEM UNTIL I HAVE OUR MAN BACK.
THAT WAS YOUR MASTER PLAN, JOAN OF ARC? YOU REALLY THINK THIS LUNATIC WOULD HAVE TRADED **MOI** FOR A FEW WORTHLESS **GIRL GRUNTS?**

YORICK?
YOU **ESCAPED?**

WELL, THAT'S A RELATIVE TERM.
BUT FORGET ABOUT ME, WHAT'S THE WORD ON MAJOR TOM AND FRIENDS?

I'M NOT SURE YET. I KNEW THE ISRAELIS WOULD TRAIL US, SO WE LED THEM TO A **FAKE** LANDING ZONE. I'M HEADED FOR THE REAL ONE NOW.

I SEE SMOKE, BUT NATALYA SAID TO EXPECT THAT.
THING DID LOOK LIKE IT WAS COMING IN PRETTY FAST THOUGH, DIDN'T IT?

OKAY, I'M COMING UP ON IT AND--
HZZZ KZACK EEEEEE

THAT'S NOT FUNNY, 355!
COME ON, KNOCK OFF THE "TO BE CONTINUED" SHIT! WHAT'S GOING ON?

HELLO?

Oldenbrook, Kansas
Now

JESUS GOD.

One Small Step
Conclusion
THEY MADE IT.
BRIAN K. VAUGHAN Writer
PIA GUERRA Penciller
JOSE MARZAN, JR., Inker
Clem Robins, Letterer Pamela Rambo, Colorist
Zylonol, Separator J.G. Jones, Cover Artist
Zachary Rau, Ass't Editor Will Dennis, Editor
Y: THE LAST MAN CREATED BY BRIAN K. VAUGHAN AND PIA GUERRA

355!

DR. MANN?!
YOU'RE SUPPOSED TO BE GUARDING THE--
NATALYA'S GOT THE ISRAELIS UNDER CONTROL. SHE TOLD ME TO GIVE YOU A HAND WITH--

THEY'RE ALIVE!

WE HAVE TO HELP THEM!
NO!

BUT THEY'VE BEEN IN ZERO GRAVITY FOR MONTHS! THEY CAN'T WALK WITHOUT--
I'LL TAKE CARE OF IT, DOCTOR!
YOU JUST STAY THE HELL BACK!

ARE YOU ALL RIGHT?
HYDRAZINE LEAK... IN THE CABIN...

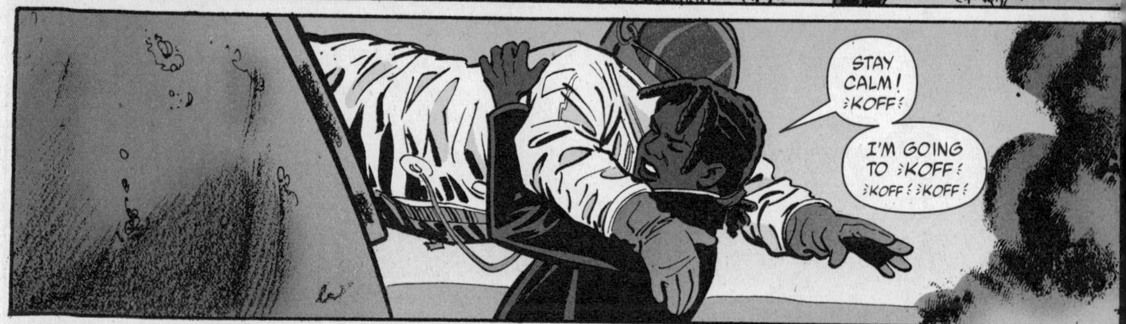

STAY CALM! KOFF
I'M GOING TO KOFF KOFF KOFF

COME ON! WE NEED TO GET THEM OUT OF HERE!
DOCTOR, I TOLD YOU--

UHF!
SHUT THE FUCK UP AND CARRY!
SLOW DOWN! WE CAN'T RISK TEARING THEIR SUITS! IF WHATEVER KILLED ALL THE MEN IS STILL IN THE ATMOSPHERE, IT COULD--

THEY SAID THERE'S A HYDRAZINE LEAK, GODDAMMIT! IF WE DON'T HURRY, THE WHOLE SOYUZ COULD--

UHF!

FUCK!
FUCK!

FUUUUCK!
355, NO!

LET GO!
HONEY, NO ONE LIVED THROUGH THAT!
THOSE PEOPLE ARE DEAD, OKAY? THEY'RE DEAD.

LET'S TAKE CARE OF THE LIVING.

IS EVERYONE OKAY? I HEARD AN **EXPLOSION.**
YORICK?

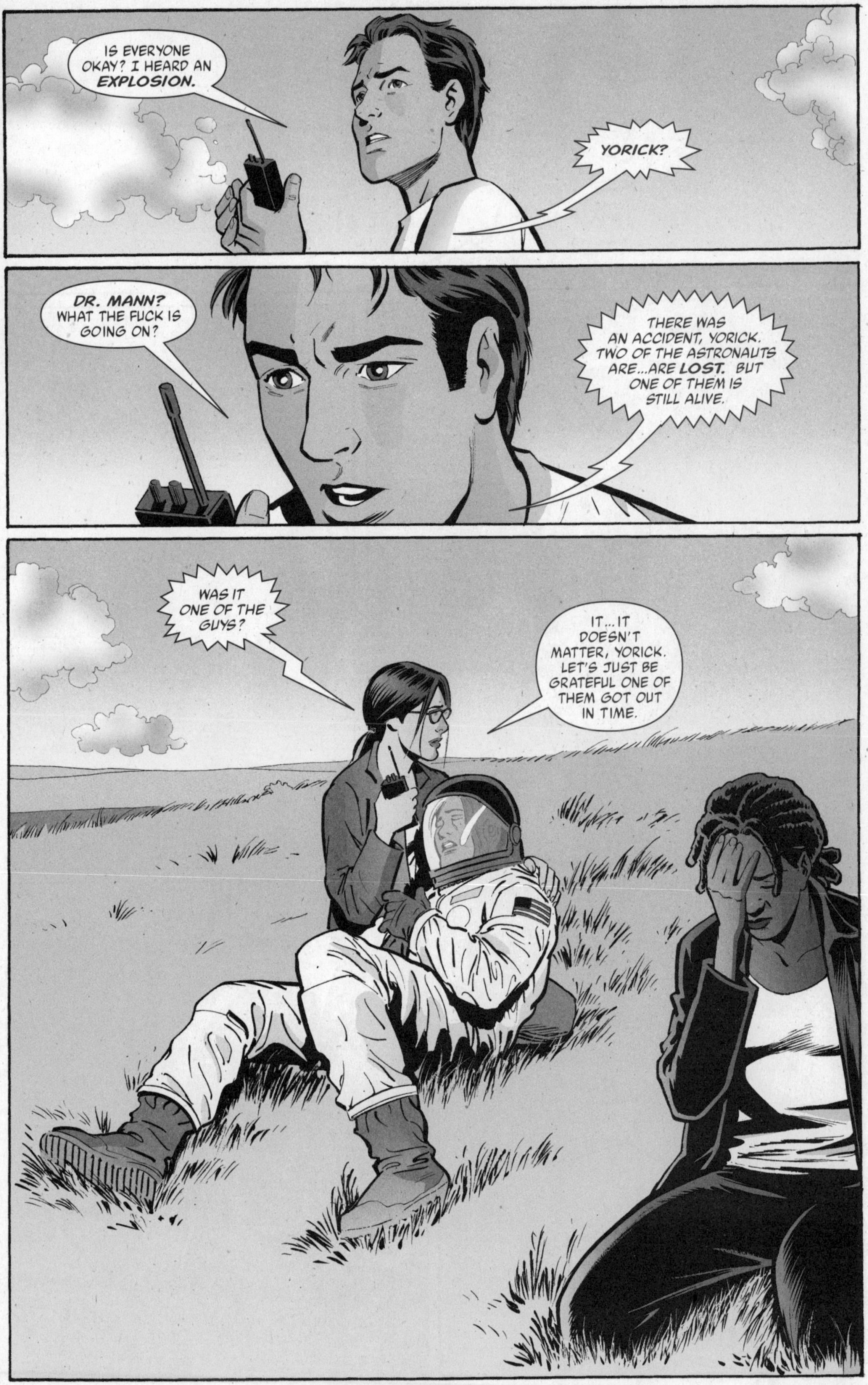

DR. MANN? WHAT THE FUCK IS GOING ON?
THERE WAS AN ACCIDENT, YORICK. TWO OF THE ASTRONAUTS ARE...ARE **LOST.** BUT ONE OF THEM IS STILL ALIVE.

WAS IT ONE OF THE GUYS?
IT... IT DOESN'T MATTER, YORICK. LET'S JUST BE GRATEFUL ONE OF THEM GOT OUT IN TIME.

WHAT DOES THAT MEAN?
IT MEANS ONLY THE FEMALE SURVIVED.

I'M SO SORRY.
THE ACCIDENT. IT WASN'T CAUSED BY ALTER... WAS IT?
GET AWAY FROM ME!

WHAT DO YOU CARE, ASSHOLE?
SADIE. MY NAME IS SADIE.
AND WHY DO YOU THINK I WAS KNOCKED OUT? I TRIED TO STOP HER. I--

DON'T!
I KICKED THE SHIT OUT OF YOUR BOSS AND I... I CAN DO THE SAME TO YOU.

IT'S NOT A WEAPON, YORICK.
IT'S A TRUCE.

IF THIS IS SOME KIND OF CHEAP PLOY...
NO. NO MORE GAMES. I'M TIRED OF PLAYING ARMY.
GO, HELP YOUR FRIENDS.

THEY ARE FRIENDS, RIGHT? NOT CAPTORS?
CAPTORS? OF COURSE NOT. WHO TOLD YOU...
IT DOESN'T MATTER. OUR INTELLIGENCE WAS POOR FOR THIS MISSION. NOT THAT IT EXCUSES OUR ACTIONS...

I PROMISE TO WAIT HERE WITH ALTER UNTIL YOUR PEOPLE DECIDE WHAT PUNISHMENT THE TWO OF US DESERVE.
I ONLY ASK THAT YOU SHOW MERCY TO THE OTHER GIRLS. THEY'RE NOT TO BLAME FOR OUR--

OH, SAVE THE A FEW GOOD MEN CRAP. ALL OF THE GOOD MEN ARE DEAD.
JUST TELL ME...WHY DID YOU PEOPLE DO THIS? AMERICA AND ISRAEL ARE SUPPOSED TO BE FRIENDS.

DON'T YOU KNOW? THIS IS WHAT HAPPENS TO FRIENDS WHEN A MAN COMES BETWEEN THEM.

ANYBODY HOME...?

AK AK AK
AHH!

OH...HEY, AMPERSAND.
NICE TO SEE YOU, TOO, BUDDY.

BUT WHAT IS THAT **SMELL** ON YOUR HANDS?
YORICK!

355.

YOU OKAY?
NOT EVEN CLOSE.
HOW'S OUR SPACE CADET?

RECOVERING DOWN IN THE HOT SUITE. DR. MANN AND THE TWINS THINK SHE'S GONNA BE FINE.
BUT YORICK, THE TWO *MEN*...
I KNOW, I HEARD. NATALYA FILLED ME IN ON THE WHOLE NIGHTMARE WHILE WE TOOK CARE OF THOSE ISRAELI SOLDIERS YOU CAPTURED.

WAIT, TOOK CARE OF THEM *HOW?*

WE MARCHED THEM BACK TO SADIE. SHE'S A TRAINED MEDIC, SO SHE CAN PATCH UP THE GIRLS YOU GUYS PUT HOLES IN.
WHO THE HELL IS SADIE?

THEIR NEW LEADER. THE OLD ONE'S BEEN HOGTIED AND COURT-MARTIALED OR WHATEVER, SO SADIE'S IN CHARGE NOW. SHE'S GOOD PEOPLE.
SHE HELPED KIDNAP YOU!
YEAH, AND THEN SHE HELPED ME ESCAPE.

SO WHAT, NOW WE'RE JUST SUPPOSED TO LET THEM GO?
WHAT CHOICE DO WE HAVE, 355? ARE WE GONNA BUILD A P.O.W. CAMP FOR THE WHOLE PLATOON?
BESIDES, NATALYA'S DESTROYING ALL OF THEIR WEAPONS AS WE SPEAK. THEY'RE BEATEN AND BROKEN, AND...AND ALL THEY CAN DO NOW IS HEAD BACK TO ISRAEL WITH THEIR TAILS BETWEEN THEIR LEGS, RIGHT?

THAT'S A PRETTY MAGNANIMOUS GESTURE COMING FROM THE GUY WHO WANTED TO LOCK UP EVERY WOMAN IN SIGHT BACK IN MARRISVILLE.
YEAH, I... I KNOW.
BUT IT WAS EITHER THAT OR LINE THEM UP IN FRONT OF A FIRING SQUAD.

AND I'VE HAD JUST ABOUT ALL THE DEATH I CAN TAKE FOR A WHILE.

BUT YORICK, THAT THING THAT ALMOST HIT THE SOYUZ...
DON'T WORRY, THAT WAS ALTER, NOT SADIE.
I TRIED TO STOP HER FROM FIRING IT, BUT I GUESS I ONLY MANAGED TO KNOCK THE MISSILE OFF COURSE.

HOLD ON, YOU TOOK DOWN A SOLDIER ARMED WITH A ROCKET LAUNCHER?
I KNOW, I'M SORRY. I SWEAR, I TRY TO STAY OUT OF TROUBLE, BUT--

YOU DON'T NEED TO APOLOGIZE, 'RICK. YOU SAVED A WOMAN'S LIFE.
WELL, THAT PRETTY MUCH DEFINES A PYRRHIC VICTORY, DOESN'T IT?
I MEAN, THE LAST TWO MEN WHO ACTUALLY HAD SOMETHING TO OFFER THE WORLD ARE GONE. NOW THE FATE OF HUMANITY IS BACK ON MY WORTHLESS SHOULDERS.

OH, KNOCK OFF THE SELF-DEPRECATING BULLSHIT.
I'M NOT SAYING I WANT YOU TO KEEP PULLING YOUR STUPID STUNTS, BUT YOU DID OKAY TODAY. YOU'RE A HERO.
CHRIST, PLEASE DON'T USE THAT WORD. IF THERE'S ONE THING I NEVER WANT TO BECOME...

OH, GOD.
YOUR SISTER. I DIDN'T MEAN...

FORGET IT.
I JUST HATE THE SOUND OF HER NAME.

RIGHT. I HAVE TO REMEMBER TO CALL THOSE SANDWICHES **SUBS,** NOT... YOU KNOW.
SMARTASS.

HEY, LET ME ASK YOU SOMETHING.
WHEN YOU WERE TRYING TO CONVINCE THE ISRAELIS TO GIVE ME BACK, AND YOU TOLD THEM THAT YOU WERE IN ***LOVE*** WITH ME, YOU...YOU DIDN'T ***MEAN*** IT, DID YOU?
NIGGA, **PLEASE.**
WHEW.
I WAS ***HOPING*** YOU'D SAY THAT.
HEH. YEAH...

DANGER!

BIOSAFETY LEVEL 4

AIR-LOCK DOOR/DECON SHOWER
NO ENTRY WITHOUT HAZMAT SUIT

DR. WEBER?
GOD, NO ONE'S CALLED ME THAT IN *MONTHS.*
CIBA IS FINE.

CIBA, I'M DR. MANN. I HELPED BRING YOU IN. MY CONDOLENCES ABOUT THE... THE...
EXCUSE ME?
THE L.O.C.V.

"LOSS OF CREW AND VEHICLE."
NASA NEVER MET A CATASTROPHE IT COULDN'T DISTILL INTO AN ACRONYM.

MY CREW-MATES. WERE YOU ABLE TO RECOVER ANY...ANY REMAINS?
NOT YET. THE TEMPERATURE OF THE BLAST...
IF IT'S ANY CONSOLATION, THEY DIED INSTANTLY.

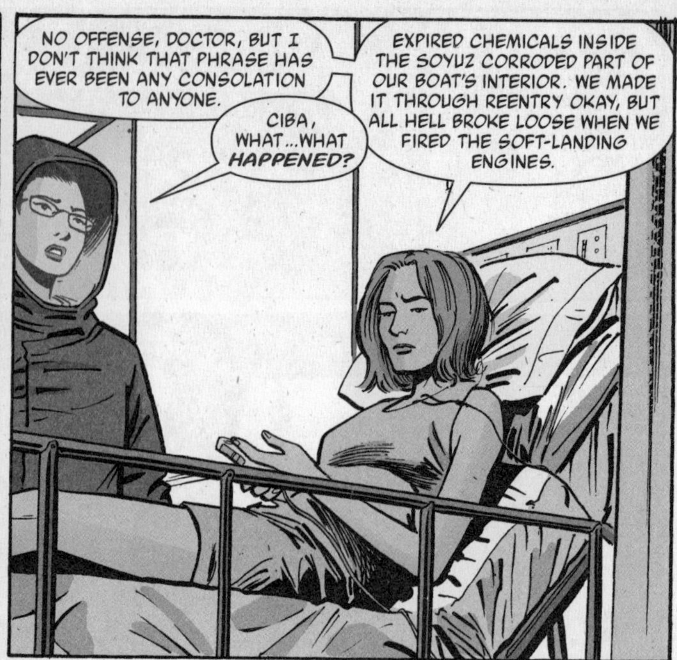
NO OFFENSE, DOCTOR, BUT I DON'T THINK THAT PHRASE HAS EVER BEEN ANY CONSOLATION TO ANYONE.
CIBA, WHAT...WHAT **HAPPENED?**
EXPIRED CHEMICALS INSIDE THE SOYUZ CORRODED PART OF OUR BOAT'S INTERIOR. WE MADE IT THROUGH REENTRY OKAY, BUT ALL HELL BROKE LOOSE WHEN WE FIRED THE SOFT-LANDING ENGINES.

I REALIZE THAT, BUT...
FORGIVE ME IF THIS IS INDELICATE, BUT YOU THREE HAD RADIO CONTACT WITH THE RUSSIANS. YOU **KNEW** ABOUT THE PLAGUE, YOU KNEW ALL OF THE MEN WERE **DEAD** DOWN HERE...
...SO WHY DID THE TWO PRECIOUS MALES ON BOARD LET A USELESS **WOMAN** ESCAPE FIRST?

I'M SORRY.
NO, BELIEVE ME, I SCREAMED THE SAME THING, BUT THE BOYS WOULDN'T LISTEN.
AS SOON AS WE BLEW THE EXPLOSIVE BOLTS ON THE HATCH, JOE AND VLAD STARTED PUSHING ME OUTSIDE. THEY KEPT SAYING THE SAME THING OVER AND OVER...

"WOMEN AND CHILDREN FIRST."

THEY JEOPARDIZED THE FUTURE OF MANKIND...FOR CHIVALRY?
NEVER.
THOSE TWO MEN WERE THE BRAVEST, MOST NOBLE...
DOCTOR, WHEN THEY SAID "WOMEN AND CHILDREN," THEY MEANT IT LITERALLY.
YOU MEAN, YOU'RE...YOU'RE PREGNANT?
YOU HAVE TO UNDER-STAND, WE WERE UP THERE FOR ALMOST A YEAR. WE WERE SCARED AND LONELY AND...AND NONE OF US REALLY THOUGHT WE WOULD MAKE IT BACK ALIVE.
JESUS, WHICH ONE IS THE FATHER?
I DON'T KNOW.
I LOVED THEM BOTH SO MUCH.
SO FUCKING MUCH...

DO WE KNOW THE SEX YET?

SHE'S ONLY THREE WEEKS ALONG, TOO EARLY TO TELL.

BUT IF HER CHILD *IS* MALE, IT SHOULD BE FINE.

YOU BROUGHT THE MOTHER INSIDE IN AN UNCOMPROMISED SUIT, SO THEY THEORETICALLY HAVEN'T BEEN EXPOSED TO ANY POSSIBLE REMNANTS OF THE PLAGUE.

...THIS IS WHY YOU WILL PLEASE BE LEAVING THEM IN THE COMPANY OF *ME.*

BECAUSE OF ISRAEL WOMENS, I NOW HAVE MANY OF BANGING ARTILLERY TO USE ON ANYONE WHO MIGHT BROUGHT TROUBLE IN.
MAN, I WOULD *LOVE* TO DIAGRAM THAT SENTENCE.

‹NATALYA, WE CAN'T ASK YOU TO STAY. YOU'VE DONE SO MUCH ALREADY. YOU DESERVE TO GO *HOME.*›
‹I APPRECIATE THE OFFER, PAL, BUT I CAN'T GO BACK TO RUSSIA, NOT EMPTY-HANDED.›
‹BESIDES, I DEDICATED MY *LIFE* TO RETRIEVING OUR LAST MAN. NOW THAT HE'S PASSED, I'M A SHIP WITHOUT A RUDDER. LOOKING AFTER THIS KID MIGHT STOP ME FROM, YOU KNOW, *CAPSIZING.*›

WHAT ABOUT ME? SOMEONE WILL HAVE TO RUN TESTS AND COLLECT GENETIC SAMPLES AND--
MY SISTER AND I ARE MORE THAN QUALIFIED TO HANDLE THAT, DR. MANN. YOU SHOULD PRESS ON TO YOUR BACKUP LAB, CONTINUE YOUR RESEARCH ON YORICK AND HIS PET.
WHAT'S THE HURRY? WE CAN STICK AROUND LONG ENOUGH TO PASS OUT CIGARS AND SHIT, CAN'T WE? THERE MIGHT BE A BOUNCING BABY *BOY* ON THE WAY!

IF THE FETUS IS MALE, WE CAN'T KEEP ALL OF OUR EGGS IN ONE BASKET...OR SPERM IN ONE BARN, AS THE CASE MAY BE.
WE HAVE TO GET YORICK OUT OF HERE ASAP.

SORRY, LADIES, I GUESS THAT'S OUR CUE. WE LIKE TO STORM INTO TOWN, INFLICT MAXIMUM DAMAGE, AND THEN DISAPPEAR...LIKE A KISS CONCERT.
ONLY WITH LESS UNINTENDED PREGNANCIES IN OUR WAKE.
HEY, IT WAS NICE OF YOU TO BRING A LITTLE EXCITEMENT OUR WAY, DOCTOR.

DOSVIDANYA, ZAMYATIN. I WISH I COULD HAVE HEARD THE STORY BEHIND THAT GOLD STAR OF YOURS.
<AND PERHAPS YOU STILL WILL.>
<UNTIL THEN, KEEP YOUR POWDER DRY AND ALL THAT.>

LATER, NATALYA. THANKS FOR, WELL, "HOPE" IS A CORNY WORD, BUT--
YOU ARE GOOD BOY, YORICK.

WHEN YOU ARE DONE, YOU MAY EVEN BE OKAY MAN.

‹I'M SORRY ABOUT THIS, ALTER, BUT IT DOES MAKE THINGS EASIER.›
‹TELL ME, SADIE, HOW DO YOU THINK THE LEGION OF WOMEN STILL LOYAL TO ME IN ISRAEL WILL HANDLE YOUR LITTLE **COUP?**›

‹I SUPPOSE WE'LL CROSS THAT BRIDGE WHEN WE MAKE IT BACK HOME... **IF** WE MAKE IT. WE STILL HAVE TO REPAIR THE TROOP TRANSPORT AND--›
‹COLONEL, SECURE FREQUENCY FOR YOU.›

‹WHAT DID WE DISCUSS, NAIM? NO MORE RANKS.›
‹SORRY, UM, **SADIE.**›
‹IT'S THE AMERICAN POLITICIAN.›

‹NO, WE'RE DONE BEING MANIPULATED BY WOMEN WHOSE POWER HAS MADE THEM **PARANOID.**›
‹SO WHAT SHOULD I DO?›
‹TELL HER WE HAVE ONLY ONE THING TO SAY TO HER...›

Washington, D.C.
Now

I...I DON'T UNDERSTAND YOUR MESSAGE. IS THAT SUPPOSED TO MEAN HELLO OR GOODBYE? OR PEACE?
PLEASE, WHERE'S ALTER? WERE YOU ABLE TO RESCUE YORICK?

I'M BEGGING YOU, TELL ME WHAT'S HAPPENED TO MY SON!
NICE TO SEE THAT YOU'RE WORRIED ABOUT ME.

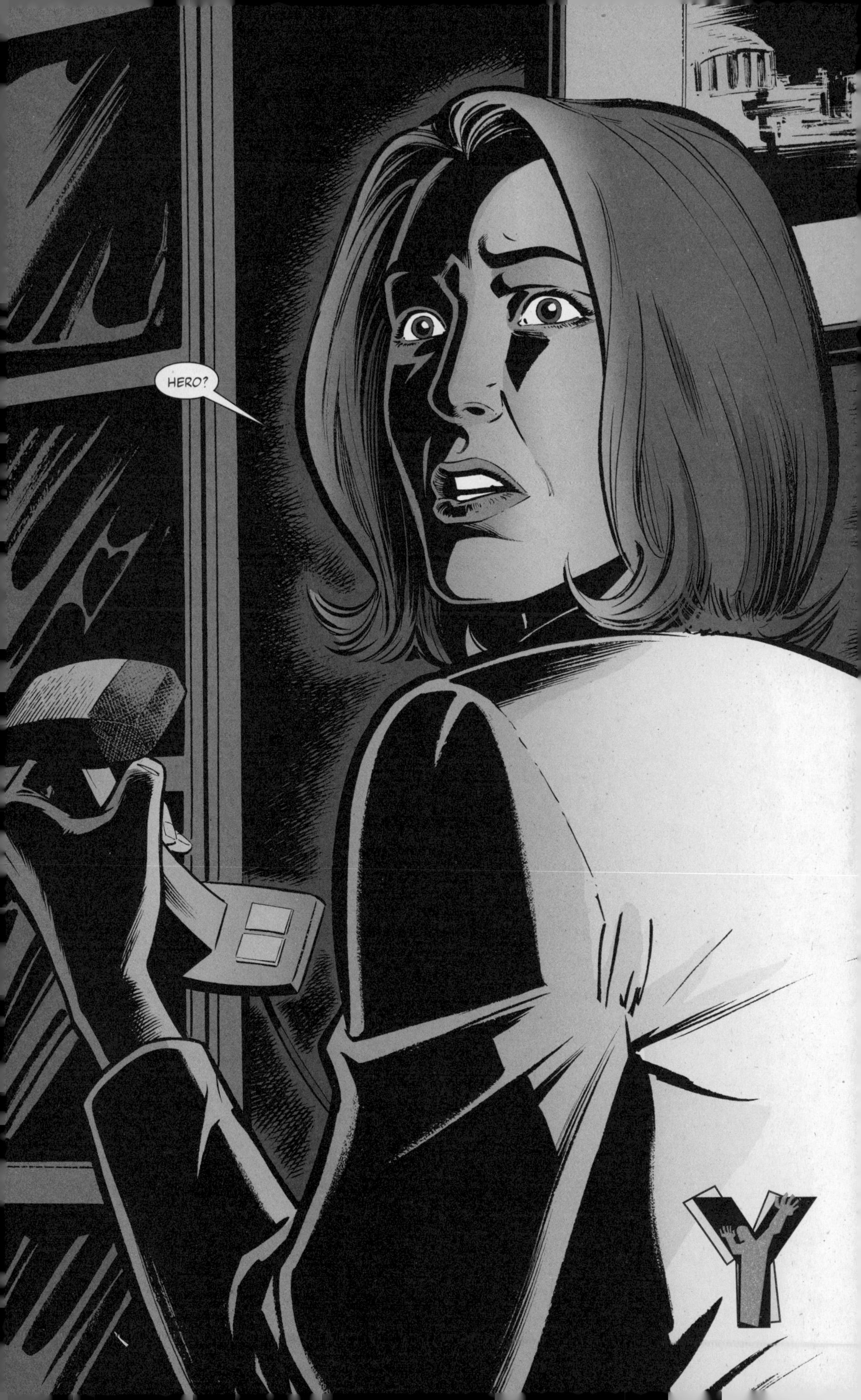
HERO?

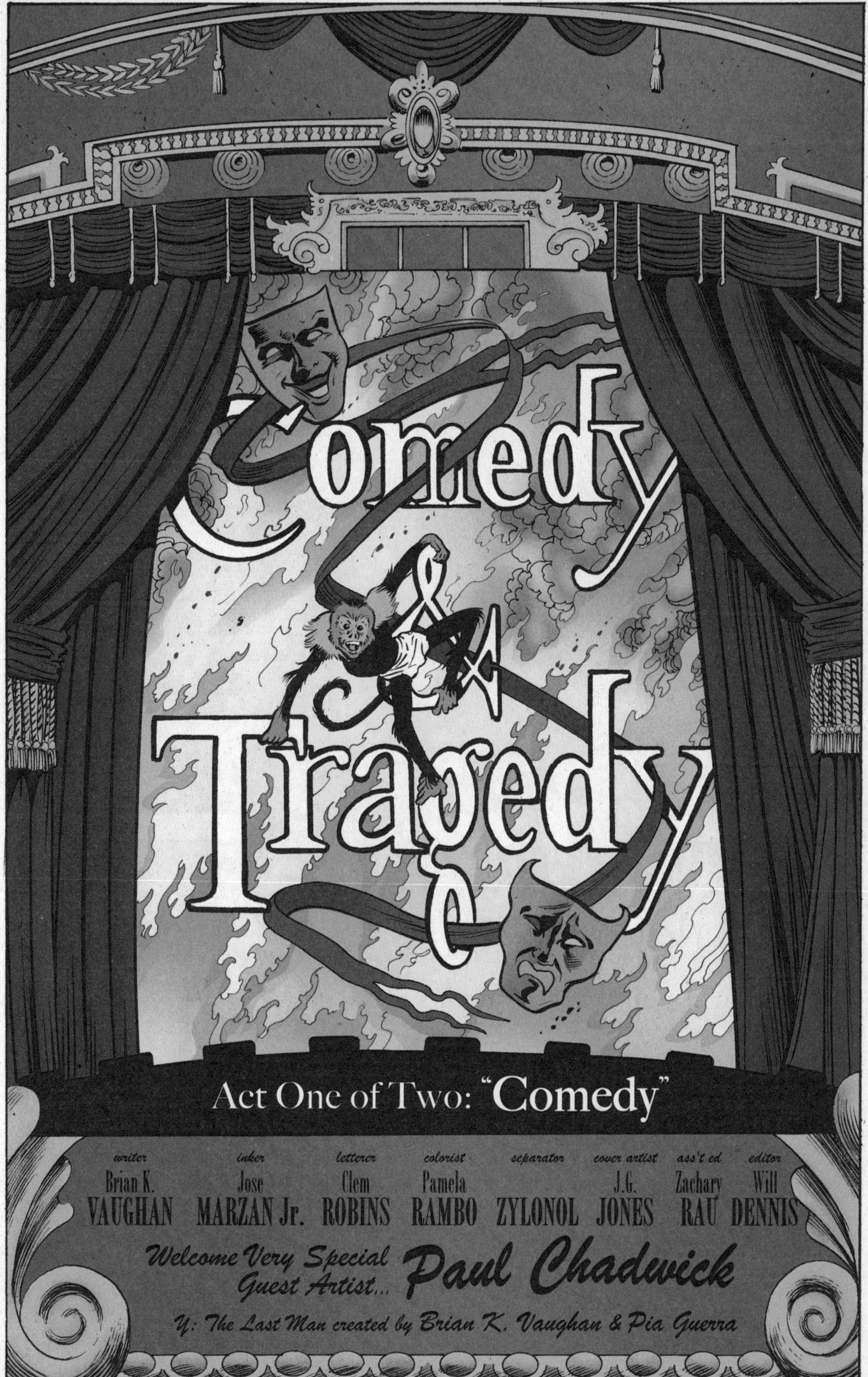
Comedy & Tragedy
Act One of Two: "Comedy"
writer
Brian K. VAUGHAN
inker
Jose MARZAN Jr.
letterer
Clem ROBINS
colorist
Pamela RAMBO
separator
ZYLONOL
cover artist
J.G. JONES
ass't ed
Zachary RAU
editor
Will DENNIS
Welcome Very Special Guest Artist... Paul Chadwick
Y: The Last Man created by Brian K. Vaughan & Pia Guerra

AT LAST I MAY ATONE, IN SOME SLIGHT MEASURE, FOR THE REPEATED ACTS OF THEFT AND PILLAGE...
...WHICH, AT A SENSE OF DUTY'S STERN DICTATION, I, CIRCUMSTANCE'S VICTIM, HAVE BEEN GUILTY!
YOUNG FREDERIC!
WHO CALLS?

YOUR LATE COMMANDER, THE PIRATE KING!
AND I, YOUR LITTLE RUTH!
OH, MAD INTRUDERS, HOW DARE YE FACE ME! 
KNOW YE NOT, OH RASH ONES, THAT I HAVE DOOMED YOU TO ***EXTERMINATION?***
HAVE MERCY ON US! HEAR US, ERE YOU SLAUGHTER!
I THINK NOT!

UHF!

AND SO...

ALL IS READY, FREDERIC, YOUR CREW AWAITS YOU!
WHAT THE...?

GOD-DAMMIT, MANDA!
YOU'RE NOT SUPPOSED TO ENTER UNTIL AFTER THE SONG!
HUH? OH, SORRY, EDIE. THIS... THIS IS MY FIRST PLAY, 'MEMBER?

WEREN'T BOTH OF YOUR FATHERS GAY?
YOU SHOULD HAVE A FUCKING GENETIC PREDISPOSITION FOR MUSICAL THEATER.
DON'T TALK ABOUT MY DADS!

HO HO, YOU REALLY WANNA TAKE ON EIGHT CREDITS OF STAGE COMBAT FROM STELLA ADLER?
TASTE IRON, SHORTIE!
KNOCK IT OFF, GIRLS!

SAVE THE CATTY SHIT FOR BROADWAY, EDIE.
THE REST OF YOU, LET'S TAKE FIVE!

SORRY, CAYCE, BUT IF WE'RE GONNA KEEP PICKING UP LITTLE ORPHAN ANNIES IN EVERY TOWN WE HIT, IT WOULD BE NICE IF ONE OF THEM COULD ACTUALLY **ACT** LIKE ANNIE.
GROW UP, EDIE.
YOU'RE JUST JEALOUS BECAUSE MANDA'S VOCAL RANGE SPANS MORE THAN **ONE OCTAVE.**

CAYCE, LUV, ARE YOU SURE ABOUT THIS FENCING BUSINESS? IT'S NOT IN THE SCRIPT, AND IT DOES STRIKE ME AS BEING RATHER... **GRATUITOUS.**
BESIDES, IT'S NOT AS IF THERE WILL EVER BE ANY **MALES** IN OUR AUDIENCE. WOMEN ARE MORE INTERESTED IN DRAMA AND ROMANCE THAN PUNCHING AND KICKING.
YOU CAN'T MAKE GENERALIZATIONS LIKE THAT, HENRIETTA! NOW THAT ALL OF THE MEN ARE GONE, WE HAVE TO START **EXPLODING** MYTHS ABOUT GENDER AND--
UM... EXCUSE ME?

ARE YOU PEOPLE THE PLAY ACTORS?
I...I WAS GIVEN A **FLYER.**

YES, MA'AM. WE'RE THE HUMBLE MEMBERS OF THE FISH & BICYCLE TRAVELING THEATER TROUPE. I'M OUR DIRECTOR AND SOMETIMES PLAYWRIGHT, CAYCE THOMAS.
YOU MUST BE THE MAYOR OF...FORGIVE ME, WHERE THE HELL ARE WE AGAIN?
NORTHLAKE. **NEBRASKA.** AND I WOULDN'T EXACTLY CALL MYSELF A MAYOR... MORE LIKE A **DEN MOTHER.** HEH.

SO, YOU FOLKS PUT ON SHOWS AND WHATNOT?
WE TRY OUR BEST. MY COMPANIONS AND I REPRESENT A CONFEDERATION OF CREATORS AND PERFORMERS WHO BANDED TOGETHER AFTER THE PLAGUE STRUCK.
WITH THE LACK OF DEPENDABLE ELECTRICITY THROUGHOUT THE COUNTRY, WE REALIZE THAT MOVIES, TELEVISION AND EVEN RADIO ARE LARGELY UNAVAILABLE, SO WE BRING OUR LO-TECH BRAND OF ART FROM TOWN TO TOWN AND--
DO YOU TAKE REQUESTS?

WOULDN'T YOU RATHER SEE SOMETHING A BIT MORE...ARTISTIC?

HOW ABOUT PIRATES OF PENZANCE?

IT'S A KICK-ASS GILBERT & SULLIVAN MUSICAL, A SATIRE ABOUT A SHELTERED YOUNG MAN WHO GETS SWEPT UP IN AN ADVENTURE WITH--

THE ONLY MUSICAL I'VE EVER SEEN IS THAT MOULIN ROUGE.

I...DIDN'T REALLY CARE FOR IT.

WELL, WE, UH, ALSO HAVE A VERY THOUGHT-PROVOKING ALL-FEMALE PRODUCTION OF MAMET'S GLENGARRY GLEN ROSS.

THAT WOULDN'T HAVE ANY SWEARS IN IT, WOULD IT?

ACTUALLY, HOW ABOUT IF WE GO AHEAD AND PICK A PLAY **FOR** YOU? I PROMISE WE'LL FIND A PERFECT FIT.
IF YOU SAY SO.
AS FOR THE COST...?

NOT TO WORRY, WE'RE A STRICTLY NON-PROFIT ORGANIZATION. ALL WE ASK IS A DONATION OF ONE CANNED FOOD ITEM PER AUDIENCE MEMBER.
AND PREFERABLY SOMETHING OTHER THAN ***CUTTLEFISH,*** PLEASE.
WE GOT STUCK WITH EIGHTY CANS OF THAT BARF DURING A RUN OF *ARCADIA* IN CHEYENNE.
OH, THAT SHOULDN'T BE A PROBLEM.
NORTHLAKE IS THE CANNING FACTORY CAPITAL OF NEBRASKA. WE HAVE ENOUGH FOOD TO LAST US UNTIL KINGDOM COME.

WHAT WE ***DON'T*** HAVE IS ENTERTAINMENT.
OUR LIBRARY'S BEEN PRETTY WELL PILLAGED, AND THE GIRLS COULD SURE USE A BIT OF AN ESCAPE.
OF COURSE, I... I UNDERSTAND.
THERE'S A SMALL PLAYHOUSE IN TOWN SQUARE. IT'S NOT MUCH, BUT WE SHOULD HAVE ENOUGH GAS TO POWER THE FOOTLIGHTS FOR A FEW NIGHTS. AS FOR ACCOMMODATIONS, I'M AFRAID WE'RE SHORT ON--

WE'RE MORE THAN HAPPY TO SLEEP UNDER THE STARS, MA'AM.
FOR NOW, LET'S SAY THAT WE'LL DEBUT THIS FRIDAY EVENING, AND PLAN FOR AN ENCORE ON SATURDAY, MAYBE A SUNDAY MATINEE IN CASE OF OVERFLOW.
MARVELOUS! GOD BLESS YOU GOOD PEOPLE FOR YOUR SERVICE! I'LL HAVE SOME OF MY HOMEMADE HOTCAKES WAITING AT THE PLAYHOUSE TOMORROW MORNING!

EXPLODING MYTHS ABOUT GENDER, EH?
YEAH... ***KA-BOOM.***

TROUBLE SLEEPING, FEARLESS LEADER?
HEY, HENRIETTA. I WAS JUST TRYING TO FIND A WAY TO MAKE OUR PENZANCE PRODUCTION MORE, I DON'T KNOW... RELEVANT.
GOOD LORD, THAT HARDLY SOUNDS LIKE A BATTLE WORTH FIGHTING.

I WAS THINKING ABOUT REPLACING OUR PIRATES WITH THOSE "DAUGHTERS OF THE AMAZON" WE KEEP HEARING ABOUT.
THE ONES WHO SUPPOSEDLY TORCHED ALL THE SPERM BANKS?
I'M NOT SURE HOW KEEN DONNA REED AND FRIENDS WOULD BE TO SEE A BUNCH OF ONE-TITTED LESBIAN WARRIORS PRANCING AROUND STAGE. BESIDES, I THOUGHT THE AMAZONS WERE JUST ANOTHER URBAN LEGEND.

YEAH...YEAH, YOU'RE PROBABLY RIGHT.
DON'T BREAK YOUR BACK FOR THESE WOMEN, CAYCE. YOU HEARD THE LADY, THEY JUST WANT A LITTLE ESCAPISM.

THAT'S ALL ANY-ONE WANTS THESE DAYS! DON'T THEY UNDERSTAND, THE ONLY WAY WE'RE EVER GOING TO ESCAPE THE ABSOLUTE FUCK-ING HORROR OF THE SITUATION WE'RE IN IS TO CONFRONT IT!
WE DON'T NEED ART THAT PACIFIES, WE NEED ART THAT CHALLENGES AND--
AIEEEEEE

EDIE!

WHAT DID YOU *DO* TO HER?

DON'T BLAME *ME,* THE BRAT WOKE US ALL UP! SHE JUST STARTED SCREAMING!

I...I HEARD A NOISE OUT THERE.

SOUNDED LIKE A *MONSTER.*

OH, PRECIOUS, IT WAS PROBABLY JUST ONE OF OUR **HORSES.**
NUH-UH! I **KNOW** WHAT HORSES SOUND LIKE!
THIS WAS SOMETHING **BAD.** I THINK IT WAS THE... THE THING THAT KILLED ALL THE BOYS.

MANDA, A **MONSTER** DIDN'T MAKE THE MEN DIE.
THEN WHAT DID?
GOD?

AH...
WE STILL DON'T **KNOW,** MANDA. NO ONE DOES.
IT'S A...A MYSTERY.

THAT'S NOT TRUE.
I KNOW WHAT CAUSED THE PLAGUE.

EDIE, BE A DEAR AND BUGGER OFF, WILL YOU?
YOU'LL GIVE THE CHILD NIGHTMARES.
WE'LL ALL SLEEP BETTER ONCE WE ACCEPT THE TRUTH.

DO YOU KNOW WHO THE MOST FAMOUS ACTRESS OF SHAKESPEARE'S LIFETIME WAS?
WHAT THE HELL DOES THAT HAVE TO DO WITH ANYTHING?
IT'S A TRICK QUESTION. THERE WERE NO ACTRESSES DURING SHAKESPEARE'S LIFETIME.

EXACTLY. WOMEN WEREN'T ALLOWED ON STAGE, SO MALES HAD TO PLAY BOTH SEXES.
NO KIDDING, EDIE, WE ALL TOOK INTRO TO DRAMA HISTORY.
THEN YOU KNOW WHAT ELSE HAPPENED DURING SHAKESPEARE'S LIFETIME.
YOU KNOW WHAT CLOSED DOWN ALL THE THEATERS AND KILLED, LIKE, MILLIONS OF PEOPLE.
THE BLACK DEATH.
BINGO. AND WHEN DID THE BLACK DEATH FINALLY DISAPPEAR?
IN 1670 ... RIGHT AFTER WOMEN WERE ALLOWED BACK ON STAGE.

WHAT ARE YOU SUGGESTING, THAT THE BLACK DEATH WAS SOME KIND OF PUNISHMENT... FOR KEEPING WOMEN OUT OF THEATER?
THINK ABOUT IT, A LOT OF ANTHROPOLOGISTS OR WHATEVER BELIEVE THAT THE FIRST PERFORMERS WERE WOMEN, RIGHT? DRAMA IS IN OUR BLOOD.
SO STOPPING US FROM ACTING IS UNNATURAL, AND SCREWING WITH THE NATURAL ORDER ALWAYS MESSES SHIT UP.

BUT WHAT ABOUT OUR PLAGUE? THERE WAS NOTHING PREVENTING ANY OF US FROM ACTING WHEN IT HAPPENED.
BULLSHIT! HOW MANY GOOD ROLES WERE OUT THERE FOR WOMEN YOUR AGE BEFORE ALL THE MEN DIED, HENRIETTA?

WELL...
HOW MANY GOOD ROLES WERE OUT THERE FOR ANY OF US? UNLESS YOU WERE NINETEEN, WILLING TO SHOW YOUR BOOBS, AND/OR JULIA ROBERTS, WHAT DID WE HAVE?
I'M NOT SAYING I'M HAPPY THAT ANYBODY CROAKED, BUT IF YOU ASK ME, THIS WHOLE CATASTROPHE WAS JUST MOTHER NATURE'S WAY OF EVENING THE SCORE.

THAT IS THE MOST OUTRAGEOUS, EGOCENTRIC, STUPID THING I HAVE EVER--
HRRRREEE

I...I THINK IT'S BACK.

HENRIETTA, GET MANDA INSIDE MY TENT. EDIE, YOU'RE WITH ME.
THE REST OF YOU, HOLD YOUR GROUND.
BOOYAH.

WHAT DO YOU THINK WE'RE DEALING WITH HERE, BOSS?
HELL IF I KNOW... THEY HAVE BANSHEES IN NEBRASKA?

HEY, ISN'T THAT A PROP GUN?
JESUS, EDIE, WHY DON'T YOU PROJECT THAT INFORMATION A LITTLE LOUDER?
RHEEEE

THERE!
WHERE?

THERE!

WHAT THE FUCKING... FUCK?
I THINK IT'S A MONKEY.
RHEE RHEEE

NO SHIT, JANE GOODALL. WHAT IS IT DOING HERE?

MUST HAVE ESCAPED FROM A ZOO.
NAH, MONKEYS DON'T WEAR **DIAPERS** AT THE ZOO.
THIS HAS GOT TO BE ONE OF THOSE HELPER MONKEYS. YOU KNOW, THE ONES DISABLED PEOPLE SOMETIMES HAVE? ITS MASTER PROBABLY DIED IN THE PLAGUE.
EREE

OH CHRIST, IT'S ***BLEEDING.***
DON'T BE SCARED, CUTIE.
CAYCE AND I ARE FRIENDS. WE'RE GONNA MAKE YOU ALL BETTER.
WE ***ARE?***
EDIE, WHAT IF THAT THING HAS RABIES OR--

THERE, THERE, BABY.
MAMA'S NOT GONNA LET ***ANY-BODY*** HURT YOU.

CRAP.
GODDAMN BIOLOGICAL CLOCKS...

OKAY, LADIES, YOU'VE ALL HAD A CHANCE TO GAWK AT OUR NEW MASCOT. CALL IS AT EIGHT A.M. SHARP TOMORROW, SO LET'S GET SOME SHUTEYE.

AND NO MORE BAD THOUGHTS TONIGHT, RIGHT, KIDDO?

I GUESS...

WHAT'S THE PROGNOSIS, DR. DOLITTLE?

MUCH BETTER NOW THAT THE BEAST AND I ARE BOTH PROPERLY ***PISSED.***

SERIOUSLY, STITCHING MONKEY FLESH BACK TOGETHER IS A WALK IN THE PARK COMPARED TO SEWING NINETEEN BLOODY ***PIRATE COSTUMES*** OUT OF THIN AIR.

WHAT DO YOU THINK HAPPENED, HANK? WAS SHE ATTACKED BY A DOG OR SOMETHING?

I SINCERELY DOUBT IT. THE CUT WAS CLEAN, BUT DEEP...LIKE SOMEONE OUT THERE TOOK A SWING AT HER WITH A ***BUTCHER'S KNIFE*** OR SOMETHING.

GREAT, SO MUCH FOR "NO MORE BAD THOUGHTS."

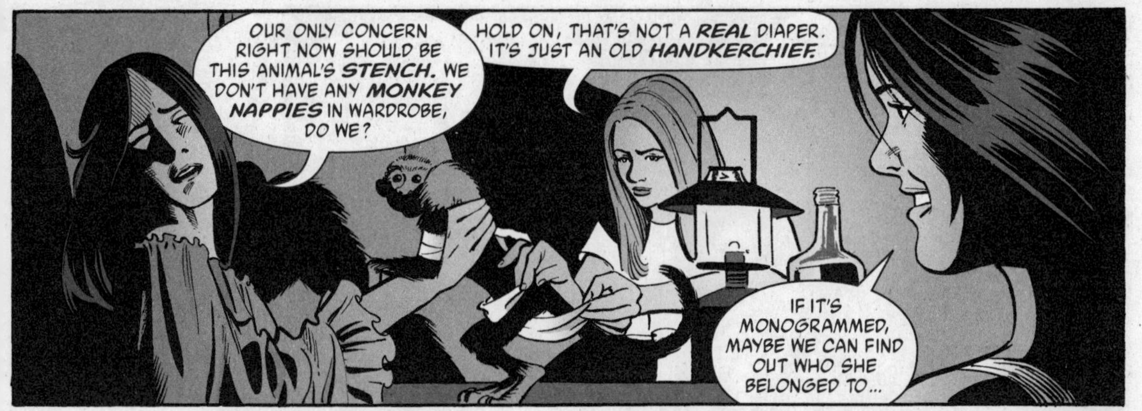
OUR ONLY CONCERN RIGHT NOW SHOULD BE THIS ANIMAL'S **STENCH.** WE DON'T HAVE ANY **MONKEY NAPPIES** IN WARDROBE, DO WE?
HOLD ON, THAT'S NOT A **REAL** DIAPER. IT'S JUST AN OLD **HANDKERCHIEF.**
IF IT'S MONOGRAMMED, MAYBE WE CAN FIND OUT WHO SHE BELONGED TO...

EWW.
UNLESS THE OWNER'S NAME WAS **BROWN,** I DON'T THINK WE'RE GOING TO FIND ANY CLUES IN HERE. POOR GIRL HASN'T BEEN CHANGED IN DAYS.

ACTUALLY, I'M NOT SO SURE THIS POOR GIRL...**IS** A GIRL.

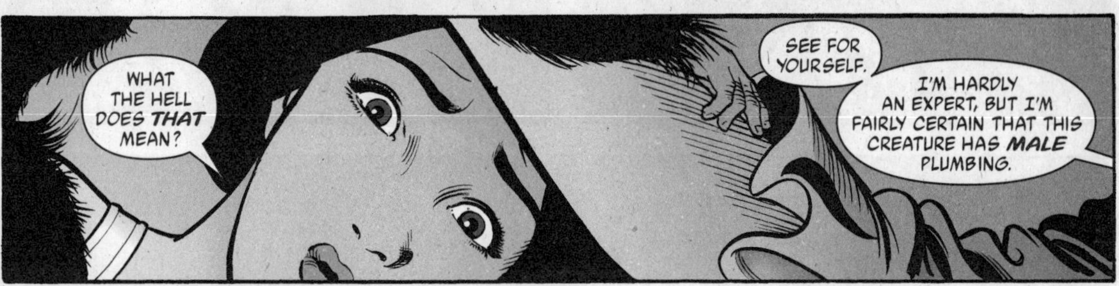
WHAT THE HELL DOES **THAT** MEAN?
SEE FOR YOURSELF.
I'M HARDLY AN EXPERT, BUT I'M FAIRLY CERTAIN THAT THIS CREATURE HAS **MALE** PLUMBING.

HOLY CRAP, SHE'S **RIGHT.**
THAT'S **IMPOSSIBLE.** MONKEYS PROBABLY JUST HAVE WEIRD ANATOMIES. MAYBE THAT'S AN ENLARGED CLITORIS OR--
EE EEE

OH.
YEAH, NEVER SEEN A LITTLE MAN IN THE BOAT DO **THAT** BEFORE.

BUT I THOUGHT THE PLAGUE KILLED EVERY MAMMAL WITH A Y CHROMOSOME. I MEAN, I LOST BOTH MY MALE CATS. AND ALL OF MY BOYFRIEND'S STALLIONS DIED.
HALF OF THE MICE IN MY APARTMENT FINALLY PASSED ON, AND I'D BEEN TRYING TO KILL THEM FOR YEARS.
SO THE PLAGUE AFFECTED EVERYTHING BUT MONKEYS? HOW THE FUCK DOES THAT MAKE ANY SENSE? ISN'T THEIR DNA, LIKE, ALMOST IDENTICAL TO OURS?

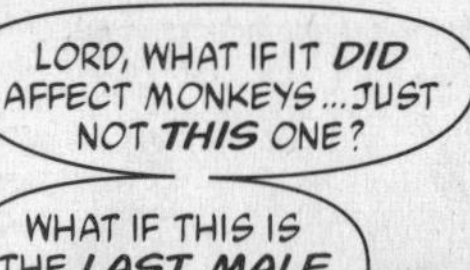
LORD, WHAT IF IT DID AFFECT MONKEYS...JUST NOT THIS ONE?

WHAT IF THIS IS THE LAST MALE ON EARTH?

YOU'RE STARTING TO SOUND LIKE EDIE, HENRIETTA.
BUBBLES HERE IS PROBABLY JUST SOME KIND OF FREAK ANOMALY...LIKE THE HANDFUL OF PEOPLE WHO ARE SUPPOSEDLY IMMUNE TO HIV INFECTION, YOU KNOW?
THAT STILL MAKES THIS AN ENORMOUS DISCOVERY. WE HAVE TO TELL--

NO! THIS STAYS BETWEEN THE THREE OF US.
IF WORD SPREADS, WOMEN MIGHT START HOLDING OUT HOPE THAT A HUMAN MALE IS ALIVE SOME-WHERE, TOO.
WHAT'S SO BAD ABOUT GIVING PEOPLE A LITTLE HOPE?

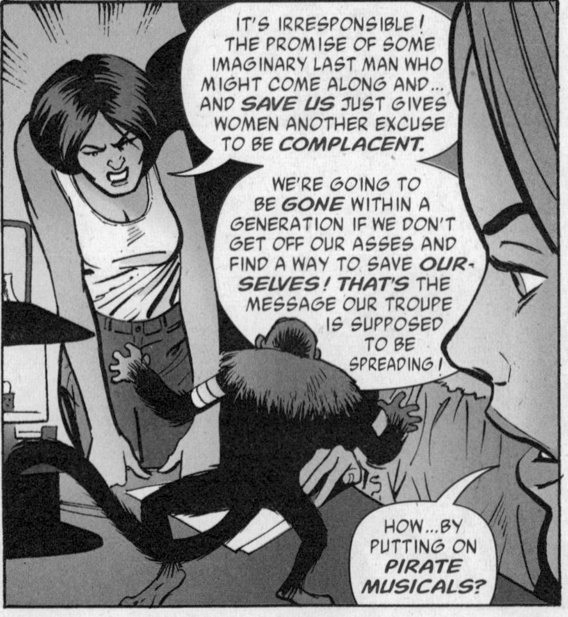
IT'S IRRESPONSIBLE! THE PROMISE OF SOME IMAGINARY LAST MAN WHO MIGHT COME ALONG AND... AND SAVE US JUST GIVES WOMEN ANOTHER EXCUSE TO BE COMPLACENT.
WE'RE GOING TO BE GONE WITHIN A GENERATION IF WE DON'T GET OFF OUR ASSES AND FIND A WAY TO SAVE OUR-SELVES! THAT'S THE MESSAGE OUR TROUPE IS SUPPOSED TO BE SPREADING!
HOW...BY PUTTING ON PIRATE MUSICALS?

I'M SORRY, CAYCE, BUT--
NO.
YOU'RE... YOU'RE ABSOLUTELY RIGHT.

SO...WE ARE GOING TO TELL THE OTHERS?
NO. WE'RE GOING TO DO A PLAY ABOUT IT.
A PLAY ABOUT A MONKEY?

A PLAY ABOUT THE LAST MAN ON EARTH.

AN ORIGINAL WORK?
WHY NOT? I'M GOING TO WRITE SOMETHING SET RIGHT HERE, RIGHT NOW...A STORY ABOUT A GROUP OF WOMEN WHO DISCOVER THE ONLY LIVING MAN.

IS THAT REALLY SUCH A GOOD IDEA, LUV? WON'T IT SEEM LIKE WE'RE EXPLOITING TRAGEDY FOR, WELL... THE PURPOSES OF ENTERTAIN-MENT?
BUT THIS WILL BE MORE THAN ENTERTAINMENT! THIS WILL BE ART! WE'LL BE USING FICTION TO...TO HELP US GET TO THE TRUTH!
IT'S THE PERFECT STORY TO CONVEY ALL OF THE IDEAS I'VE BEEN TRYING TO GET ACROSS ABOUT LIFE IN THE POST-PLAGUE WORLD!

IT'S LIKE THE GODS SENT ME MY OWN SMELLY LITTLE MUSE.
AND YOU CALL ME EGOCENTRIC...

TRUST ME, EDIE, THIS PLAY IS GOING TO BE A FUCKING **SENSATION.**

PEOPLE WILL COME FROM **ALL OVER** TO SEE IT!

ROXY
THE LAST MAN
APPEARING
TONIGHT ONLY

Afternoon.

A Kitchen: A table, a chair, a jar of pickled artichoke hearts.

ARTICHOKE HEARTS

A lone figure enters.

This is **TERESA**, one of billions of women made a widow by the Plague.

But unlike so many of her friends, Teresa hasn't turned to drugs or alcohol, she hasn't contemplated suicide. She is a pillar of strength, an independent woman.

Because Teresa and her husband built a shelter in their basement after 9/11, she has enough food to last her more than a year.
RTICH EARTS
Teresa will not die. She is a **survivor.**

But as she sits down to enjoy her lunch, Teresa is confronted with a problem…

She is unable to open the jar.
She strains and struggles, but to no avail.

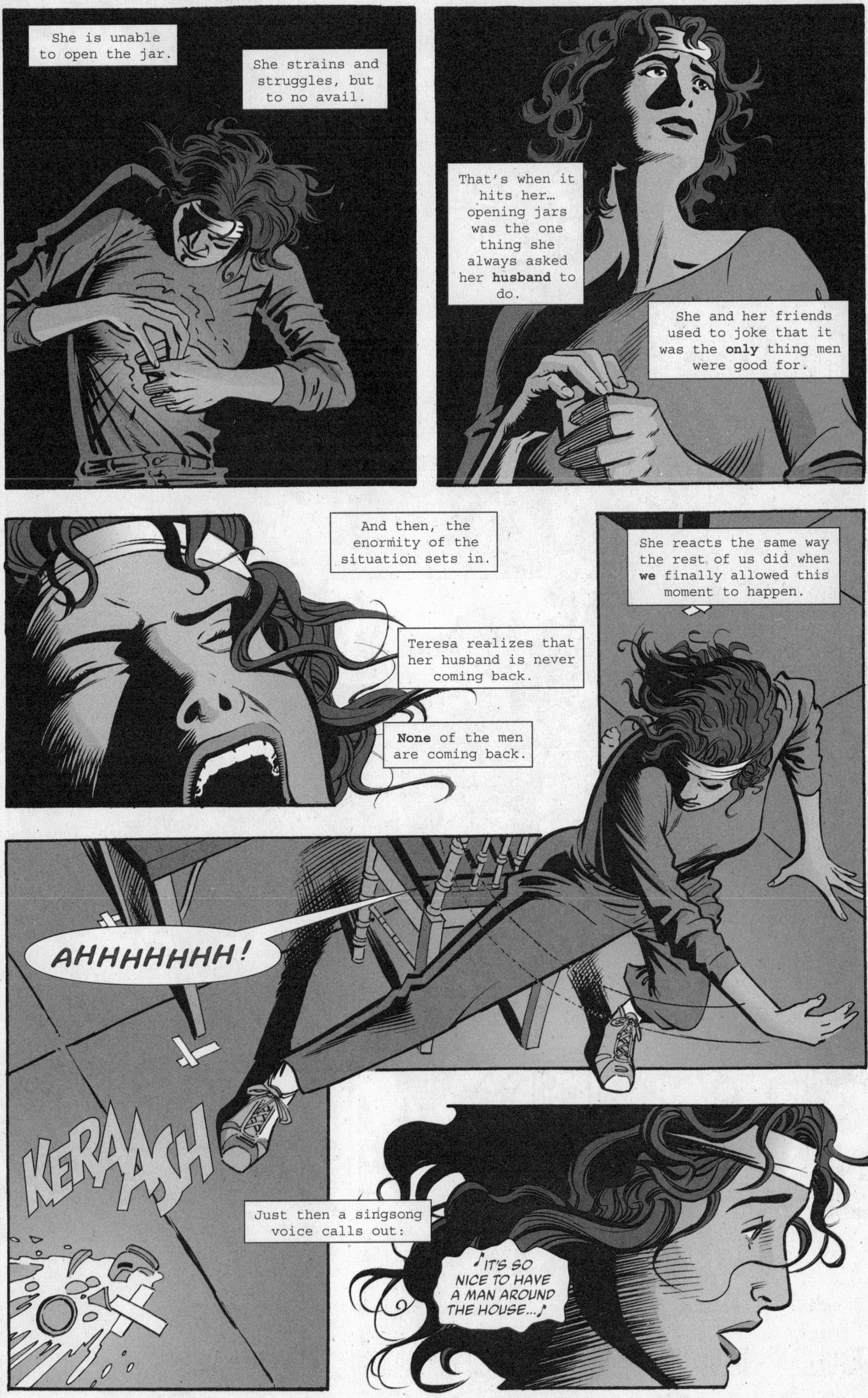

That's when it hits her... opening jars was the one thing she always asked her **husband** to do.
She and her friends used to joke that it was the **only** thing men were good for.

And then, the enormity of the situation sets in.

Teresa realizes that her husband is never coming back.

None of the men are coming back.

She reacts the same way the rest of us did when **we** finally allowed this moment to happen.

AHHHHHHH!

KERAASH

Just then a singsong voice calls out:

♪IT'S SO NICE TO HAVE A MAN AROUND THE HOUSE...♪

Enter LIONEL, the husband Teresa thought was dead!
LIONEL?
THE LAST MAN ON EARTH IS NAMED LIONEL?

COMEDY & TRAGEDY

Act Two of Two: "&"

writer Brian K. VAUGHAN *penciller* Paul CHADWICK *inker* Jose MARZAN Jr. *letterer* Clem ROBINS *colorist* Pamela RAMBO *separator* ZYLONOL *cover artist* J.G. JONES *ass't ed* Zachary RAU *editor* Will DENNIS

Y: The Last Man created by Brian K. Vaughan & Pia Guerra

SORRY, CAYCE, BUT IT'S A MILLION FUCKING DEGREES IN HERE.

AND SERIOUSLY, IS THERE ANY CHANCE MY CHARACTER'S NAME COULD BE A LITTLE MORE...DRAMATIC? HOW ABOUT SOMETHING SHAKESPEARIAN? LIKE HAMLET OR...OR ROMEO!

IF THERE'S ONE THING I HATE, IT'S CRAPPY WORKS OF FICTION THAT TRY TO SOUND IMPORTANT BY STEALING NAMES FROM THE BARD.

BESIDES, LIONEL IS MY TRIBUTE TO THE FOUNDING MOTHER OF SCI-FI...A LITTLE TIP OF THE HAT TO MARY SHELLEY.

THE FRANKENSTEIN CHICK?
BACK IN THE 1800'S, SHE WROTE THIS BOOK CALLED THE LAST MAN, ABOUT A TWENTY-FIRST CENTURY PLAGUE THAT KILLS EVERYONE EXCEPT FOR A GUY NAMED LIONEL.
FUCK... WHAT CAUSED IT?
THE PLAGUE? SHE NEVER REALLY GETS AROUND TO EXPLAINING IT. BUT IT'S NOT THE POINT OF HER STORY.
IT'S A CONDEMNATION OF THE... THE UNCHECKED MASCULINITY THAT WAS ALWAYS THREATENING TO DESTROY THE PLANET.
IT'S ABOUT THE FAILURE OF ART AND IMAGINATION TO SAVE THE WORLD.
WELL, THAT'S ALL VERY NICE, BUT I STILL DON'T UNDERSTAND MY CHARACTER'S MOTIVATION.
I MEAN, IF TERESA CAN'T OPEN THE JAR, WHY DOESN'T SHE JUST USE A PAIR OF LATEX DISHWASHING GLOVES? YOU GET A REAL NICE GRIP THAT WAY, AND IT MAKES IT SUPER-EASY TO--
NO KIDDING! BUT THIS ISN'T THE GODDAMN MARTHA STEWART HOUR! WE'RE NOT HERE TO GIVE HELPFUL HOUSEHOLD TIPS! THIS IS DRAMA! TERESA'S DILEMMA IS AN ALLEGORY!
JESUS, WHY IS EVERYONE ACTING LIKE THIS IS THEIR FIRST FUCKING PLAY?
CAYCE, LUV, PERHAPS NOW WOULD BE A GOOD TIME FOR A SHORT BREAK? YOU COULD PROBABLY DO WITH SOME FRESH AIR.
...FINE.
BUT SOMEBODY SWEEP UP THOSE ARTICHOKES. MAYBE CURIOUS GEORGETTE HERE CAN EAT THEM FOR LUNCH.
MM MNN

CAYCE, BE GENTLE WITH THE GIRLS. THEY'VE BEEN WORKING TO GET OFF-BOOK ALL MORNING.

FOR GOD'S SAKE, YOU WROTE THIS PIECE IN LESS THAN A **NIGHT.**

I DIDN'T WRITE IT, HENRIETTA. IT WROTE ITSELF.

EXACTLY. YOU'VE BEEN ACTING LIKE A WOMAN POSSESSED EVER SINCE WE FOUND THIS ANIMAL. HE'S TURNED YOU INTO--

SHHHH!

RIGHT NOW, YOU, EDIE AND I ARE THE ONLY THREE PEOPLE ALIVE WHO KNOW THAT OUR MONKEY IS ACTUALLY A **HE.**

IF ANYONE ELSE FINDS OUT THAT WE STUMBLED ONTO A LIVING **MALE,** MASS HYSTERIA WILL SWEEP THROUGH NEBRASKA LIKE A FUCKING--

WHAT IS GOING **ON** HERE?

YOU'RE DOING A PLAY ABOUT A MAN WHO SURVIVED THE PLAGUE?

THAT'S RIGHT, MA'AM. WE--
WHEN I AGREED TO LET YOU PEOPLE USE OUR THEATER, YOU TOLD ME THAT YOU WOULD FIND SOMETHING APPROPRIATE TO PERFORM.
WELL, WHAT IN HEAVEN'S NAME IS APPROPRIATE ABOUT YOUR IDEA? OUR SUFFERING SHOULDN'T BE FODDER FOR YOUR...YOUR CRUEL FLIGHTS OF FANCY!

PERHAPS YOU MIGHT WAIT TO SEE THE SHOW BEFORE YOU PASS JUDGMENT?
I DON'T NEED TO! THE WOMEN OF NORTHLAKE WANT OLD-FASHIONED ENTERTAINMENT, NOT THIS KIND OF CRASS EXPLOITATION!

REALLY? BECAUSE THE FIRST TWO EVENINGS OF THIS "CRASS EXPLOITATION" ARE ALREADY COMPLETELY SOLD OUT.
I ASSURE YOU, WE HAVE NO INTENTION OF DISRESPECTING THE FATHERS, HUSBANDS, SONS AND BROTHERS THAT YOU--THAT WE--ALL LOST.
THIS IS A PROVOCATIVE PLAY, BUT IT'S ALL DONE IN VERY GOOD TASTE.

WHAT IN THE WORLD IS TASTEFUL ABOUT THIS?
The Fish & Bicycle Traveling Theater Troupe proudly presents
THE LAST MAN
A Play By Cayce Thomas

WHAT THE FU--
ER, THAT WAS EDIE'S DOING, CAYCE. SHE THOUGHT A PICTURE OF YOUR NEW PET WOULD MAKE FOR AN INTRIGUING **TEASER POSTER.**

THESE ARE PLASTERED ALL OVER TOWN!
THIS IS HOW YOU HONOR OUR DEAD... BY COMPARING MEN TO A SMILING **CHIMP?**
OF COURSE NOT. SEE, THIS MONKEY IS SORT OF THE...THE **SYMBOL** OF OUR THEATER COMPANY. IN CHINA, THEY REPRESENT, UH, CREATIVITY AND--

WE'RE NOT INTERESTED IN YOUR PRETENTIOUS GARBAGE.
WHY DON'T YOU PEDDLE YOUR **FILTH** ELSEWHERE?

BECAUSE WE HAVE A **RIGHT** TO EXPRESS OURSELVES.

AS DO I.
AND I HAVE EVERY INTENTION OF DOING JUST THAT.

WHAT DOES **THAT** MEAN?
IGNORE HER, CAYCE.
WHEN I DID THAT PLAY ABOUT A GAY JESUS, EVERY BLOODY SOCCER MOM WITH A PLACARD CAME OUT TO--
ARK ARK ARK

WHAT'S HIS PROBLEM?
I DON'T KNOW. HE WOKE ME UP THREE TIMES LAST NIGHT BARKING LIKE THAT.
I THINK HE CAN SMELL ALL THE **BAD REVIEWS** HEADED OUR WAY...

Opening Night
Eleven Hours Later

CLAP
CLAP
CLAP
CLAP
CLAP
CLAP

WELL, THIS IS GOING BETTER THAN EXPECTED.

AND NARY A SINGLE PROTESTOR OUTSIDE.

WE'RE NOT OUT OF THE WOODS YET. I MEAN, WE'RE STILL GIVING THE AUDIENCE WHAT THEY WANT. WAIT FOR US TO START ***SUBVERTING*** THEIR FANTASIES AFTER INTERMISSION...

GOOD SHOW OUT THERE, EDIE. YOU SOUND MORE LIKE A MAN THAN LEO DICAPRIO EVER DID.

WHATEVER, I'M DONE KISSING CHICKS IN PLAYS, THAT'S FOR SURE. MY CO-STARS KEEP "ACCIDENTALLY" SLIPPING ME THE TONGUE.

CAN YOU BLAME THEM? YOU'RE ALMOST CONVINCING ENOUGH TO MAKE ***ME*** WET... AND I'M THE ONE WHO SPIRIT-GUMMED THAT THING TO YOUR FACE.

NNN

SERIOUSLY, THIS IS ACTUALLY THE BEST I'VE FELT ABOUT A ROLE IN FOREVER, CAYCE. WE SHOULD THINK ABOUT TAKING THIS ONE ON THE ROAD.

YES, BREAK A LEG OUT THERE, LUV.

LET'S SEE IF WE CAN SURVIVE ACT TWO FIRST, ALL RIGHT?

target identity - CONFIRMED

IF ANYONE ELSE TRIES TO FRENCH ME, I'LL BREAK A LOT MORE THAN ***THAT!***

‹DR. M, THIS IS TOYOTA.›
‹I'M AFRAID WE HAVE A PROBLEM.›
‹YOU'VE LOST THE ANIMAL AGAIN?›
‹NO, I'M RIGHT THE FUCK ON TOP OF IT. UNFORTUNATELY, SO ARE A BUNCH OF CIVVIES... PRETTY MUCH PERPETUALLY.›
‹I CAN RETRIEVE THE PACKAGE, BUT I CAN'T GUARANTEE THAT I WON'T OFF A FEW FRIENDLIES IN THE PROCESS.›
‹**DAMMIT.** THE LAST THING I NEED IS MORE **BLOOD** ON MY HANDS...›

‹STILL, I CAN'T GUARANTEE THAT WHATEVER GENETIC MATERIAL YOU WERE ALREADY ABLE TO CARVE OUT OF THE BEAST WILL BE ENOUGH.›
‹STAY IN POSITION FOR ANOTHER HOUR, TOYOTA. BUT ONLY MAKE A MOVE IF YOU CAN LIMIT THE NUMBER OF CASUALTIES TO NO MORE THAN ONE. I CAN'T JUSTIFY ANOTHER BODY COUNT.›
HAI, DOMO ARIGATO...

‹...YOU TIME-WASTING ASSHOLE.›
‹IF THERE'S ONE THING I HATE SITTING THROUGH, IT'S FUCKING THEATER...›

GET AWAY FROM ME! *PLEASE!*

I'M JUST TRYING TO GET TO MY WIFE!

FORGET HER, TAKE *ME!* YOU CAN FUCK MY TITS!

NO, TAKE ME! YOU CAN FUCK MY *MOUTH!*

NO, TAKE ME! YOU CAN FUCK MY--

BOOOOO!

AH, HELL.

WHAT *NOW...?*

I'VE SEEN ENOUGH!

THIS PLAY IS A MOCKERY!
SIT DOWN!
NO, SHE'S RIGHT!
IT'S OBSCENE!
BE QUIET!

ARE WE REALLY GOING TO LET THESE PEOPLE PORTRAY WOMEN AS PETTY, VICIOUS TRAMPS?
YOU JUST INTERRUPTED MY FIGHT SCENE...

...YOU FUCKING BITCH!

UHN!

EDIE, STOP IT!

EVERY-ONE, CHILL THE FUCK OUT!
NOW!
WHAT THE HELL IS THIS?
THE DEUS EX MACHINA?
‹OH, FUCK THIS LOW-PAYING BULL-SHIT.›
‹I'M OUTTA HERE...›

LISTEN UP!
WE'RE LOOKING FOR THE CAPUCHIN MONKEY PICTURED HERE!
The Fish & Bicycle Traveling Theater Troupe proudly presents
THE LAST MAN
A Play By Cayce Thomas

WHY?
WHO ARE YOU PEOPLE?

WE'RE WITH W.H.O.
THAT'S RIGHT, THE WORLD HEALTH ORGANIZATION.
WHO?

AW, YOU GOT TO IT TOO FAST, 355. YOU WERE FOUR LINES AWAY FROM AN ABBOTT AND COSTELLO ROUTINE.
THAT ANIMAL IS A PUBLIC HEALTH RISK.
I'LL HAVE TO ASK YOU TO GIVE IT BACK TO US.

ABSOLUTELY NOT!
WE PATCHED UP WHATEVER YOU MONSTERS DID TO HIM. HE BELONGS TO US NOW.
HE?

OH. IT'S NOT REALLY A BOY.
IT'S A, UH, FEMALE WITH MALE GENITALIA... LIKE THAT ACTRESS, **WHAT'S-HER-NAME.**

I BEG YOUR PARDON!
WHICH ACTRESS WOULD **THAT** BE?

OH, NOT ONE OF **YOU,** THE ONE FROM ALL THOSE HORROR--
WHAT MY ASSOCIATE **MEANT** TO SAY IS THAT WE'VE BEEN WORKING ON GENETICALLY ENGINEERING A NEW BREED OF, UH...PLAGUE-RESISTANT **HERMAPHRODITES.**
UNFORTUNATELY, THE SPECIMENS WE'VE CREATED SO FAR--LIKE THE MONKEY THAT ESCAPED OUR FACILITY--MIGHT ALSO BE CARRIERS OF A...A HIGHLY CONTAGIOUS **ASIAN FLU.**

OH.

IN THAT CASE...

WELCOME BACK, SHIT-SLINGER.

THAT'S THE LAST TIME WE TRUST **YORICK** TO KEEP AN EYE ON YOU.
HEY, I **TOLD** YOU, DR. MANN, WHEN I WOKE UP, AMPERSAND'S TRAVELING CASE WAS EMPTY, AND SOME **NINJA CHICK** WAS JUMPING OUT OF OUR TRAIN CAR.
NINJA CHICK. RIIIGHT...

THANK YOU FOR YOUR COOPERATION.
I APOLOGIZE FOR INTERRUPTING YOUR... PERFORMANCE.
HEY, IS THIS PLAY REALLY ABOUT THE LAST GUY ON EARTH?

DON'T WORRY, MA'AM, WE'VE ALREADY SHUT IT DOWN.
WHY DON'T I SHUT DOWN YOUR FAT **FACE,** DOUCHE NOZZLE?

YES, THIS WORK DOES INDEED DEAL WITH A GENTLEMAN SURVIVOR, AND THE PRODUCTION IS GOING TO HAVE A LONG, SUCCESSFUL RUN IN EVERY **OPEN-MINDED** CITY IN THE COUNTRY.
CAYCE HERE IS THE AUTHOR.

I WAS JUST WONDERING...HOW DOES IT END?

COME ON, WE DON'T HAVE TIME TO...
WAIT, I NEED TO KNOW, DOES IT HAVE A ***HAPPY*** ENDING?
OF COURSE. THE LAST MAN SAVES THE WORLD.
REALLY?
HOW?
BY COMMITTING SUICIDE, AND LETTING THE WOMEN SAVE THEMSELVES.

EVERYONE'S
A CRITIC...